WHAT'S HAPPENING TO MY WORLD?

What's Happening to My World?

Standing Against the Forces that Threaten Your Children, Your Marriage, Your Neighbors—and Your Sanity

Dee Jepsen

VINE
BOOKS

Servant Publications
Ann Arbor, Michigan

Vine Books is an imprint of Servant Publications especially
designed to serve Evangelical Christians.

Published by Servant Books
P.O. Box 8617
Ann Arbor, Michigan 48107

Cover design

89 90 91 92 93 94 10 9 8 7 6 5 4 3 2

Printed in the United States of America
ISBN 0-89283-626-1

Library of Congress Cataloging-in-Publication Data

Jepsen, Dee, 1934-
    What's happening to my world? : understanding the forces
that threaten your children, your marriage, your neighbors—
and your sanity / by Dee Jepsen.
        p. cm.
    ISBN 0-89283-626-1
    1. Christian life—1960   2. Christianity—20th century.
3. United States—Moral conditions.   4. Jepsen, Dee, 1934-
5. Christianity and Politics.   I. Title.
BV4501.2.J44   1989
277.3'0828—dc19   88-36647
                                                        CIP

Contents

Foreword

ILLUSION MUST ALWAYS BE FOLLOWED by disillusion. *What's Happening to My World?* takes us by the hand and leads us out of the pervasive moral confusion of our worlds. Dee Jepsen sees the disillusionment which is breaking in upon the distorted American Dream. Having known and worked with Dee Jepsen on several occasions, I anticipated that this book would be written in her "rolled-up-sleeves" style. These pages do not present theories for restoring our world, but rather they proclaim a call to recapture the truth needed to avoid personal, family, or, God forbid, national calamity.

Personally, I am grateful that Dee has written in plain English for the average person. Her insights, gathered from years of travel and public service, allow her to see into a nation and a society which have broken loose from their needed guidelines. Her answers are biblical and direct, like a doctor's prescription for the medicine necessary to heal a critically ill patient.

It is refreshing as well to see Dee's courage and to benefit from her feminine insight and convictions that are badly needed by the women of our day. Dee's love for God and her obvious burden and concern for others open us to hear her exhortation and warning. Her compassion for the lost and hurting activates our wills and emotions so we can respond compassionately to our suffering world.

My conviction is that *What's Happening to My World?* provides us with a biblical worldview that is the only antidote for the increasing disillusionment we see all around us. May I encourage you to read it and catch the vision.

Bob Mumford

Introduction

THE FUNDAMENTAL MESSAGE OF THIS BOOK is one of hope. Yes, there is hope in the midst of the darkness of our world. And *your* life can give expression to that hope.

As a matter of daily routine, millions of Americans read their newspapers and watch television newscasts. We witness the coverage of a variety of happenings—some mundane, many very alarming, even bizarre. They have become familiar to us. Twenty years ago, viewers would have watched in shocked disbelief what is broadcast daily through our media. But today, many Americans have become desensitized and are no longer shocked by the shocking, no longer outraged by the outrageous. Yet some of us are greatly disturbed by the conditions we see. We realize that we must do something about the darkness that surrounds us before it overtakes us completely and we, too, grow numb.

When something particularly jolting happens many of us sit perplexed and wonder, "What is happening to my world?" We recognize that there is a problem, but we do not understand what it is— much less what the solution might be. In our search for understanding, we must first look long and hard at the confusion and distress around us before we are able to apply remedies that will truly restore stability to our world. In this book I have tried to give a cursory overview of some of the nonsensical, illogical, and outlandish attitudes responsible for the instability of our world. These attitudes are often so insidious that we hardly recognize their destructive power, the way they have crept into our lives and turned our world upside down.

What's Happening to My World? is a book about coming to our senses, much as the prodigal son did as he wiped the mud of the pigpen from his eyes and determined to go back from whence he came—back to his father's house. After leaving his father's house, squandering his inheritance, and sharing food with pigs, "he came to himself." He looked around in amazement and disbelief and asked himself, "What in the world am I doing here?"

Crises of this nature have a way of creeping up on us, easing in bit by bit, sometimes through a series of wrong choices or simply through apathetic living. Before we even realize it we are in a position we would have never purposefully chosen or desired.

A frog, so it is said, will peacefully allow himself to be scalded to death. If placed in a pan of tepid water, which is then slowly heated, the passive, oblivious frog hardly notices the increase. Before it dawns on him that he should leap to safety, he is cooked to death. He does not realize the danger until it is too late. Danger crept up on him degree by degree.

We humans have succumbed also, a little at a time,

to beguiling delusions. Now danger is upon us. When we stop to look around, we can see conditions which should alarm us and spring us into action. Some of us are already numb, and others of us have no idea what to do except yell "danger!" Should we be alerted that our house is on fire, running around in circles and hollering will not quench the flames. We need to know where the fire extinguisher is and how to use it properly.

Today the danger has only one solution and that is the truth of our Creator. God has the power to bring real and lasting salvation to our lost and suffering world. He holds it out to all of us who see the danger and long to do something about it.

G.K. Chesterton wisely stated, "Tolerance is a virtue of the man without conviction." Some Christians have used the word "tolerance" to excuse inaction and moral compromise. We have sold our inheritance—the life-giving truth of God—for personal comfort, for a life without conflict. My prayer is that we will come to ourselves and realize who we are—children of the living God—and where our salvation lies. As prodigals, we must stop squandering our lives and return to our Creator who has the power to restore what has been destroyed and to bring hope to all who are in distress.

The prodigal realized his present condition as one of degradation, beneath his calling. So should we. His father rejoiced to see his son coming home to him and ran to meet him. He put a royal robe upon his son's shoulders and a ring upon his son's finger, signifying his rightful place and authority. And his father killed the fatted calf and led all his household in celebrating, for the one who was lost had been found. So will our Father in heaven celebrate our return when we come to him in repentance and faith.

We have a loving, forgiving, and wise Father who awaits our return. He longs for us to recognize who we are. We have royal blood in our veins if we are of his household. He desires for us to use his authority which is our inheritance.

We live in a world poisoned by its own sinful rebellion, suffering from the "wisdom" of man without God. We were created for something much better than a pigpen. Our Father's plan is for us to reflect his glory to a lost world. We are to make the kingdom visible through our lives. We are ambassadors to the world. What a high calling! What a tremendous opportunity! Will we leap out of the threatening darkness into the light of his truth? Come, let us embrace the great privilege of being light-bearers to our world.

ONE

Through the Looking Glass

Woe to those who call evil good, and good evil;
Who substitute darkness for light and light for
  darkness;
Who substitute bitter for sweet, and sweet for bitter!
                                                    (Is 5:20)

Once upon a time, in a land far away . . .
That is how fairy tales start. Some fairy tales are
happy stories. Some are sad. Some are scary. A few
are absurd. But they all have one thing in common:
they are "just pretend." They are not real. They have
never really happened.

In this book, we are going to look at a story that
sounds like a fairy tale. It has several of the required
elements. It is even absurd. It is certainly scary. The
scariest part of all is that it is real. It is happening
right now, every day, in the world in which you and I
live.

Accepting the Unacceptable

We all remember the story of Alice in Wonderland, the adventurous little girl with the long blond hair and the overactive imagination. She followed the White Rabbit into a bizarre world where the Mad Hatter, the March Hare, the Queen of Hearts, and dozens of other nonsensical characters lived.

So many odd things happened in Wonderland that before long Alice started behaving oddly along with everyone else. She grew so accustomed to that topsy-turvy world that she began to accept the unacceptable. Indeed, "Alice had got so much into the way of expecting nothing but out-of-the-way things to happen that it seemed quite dull and stupid for life to go on the common way" (*Alice in Wonderland,* Ch. 1).

We and Alice, it seems, have much in common.

There is great distortion in our world today, just as there was in Alice's Wonderland. Without realizing it, many of us have been taken in, just as Alice was. We have grown accustomed to the absurd, the illogical, the unacceptable. We have grown to expect "out-of-the-way" things to happen. When they do, we simply go on our way, without even calling them into question.

A Topsy-Turvy World

Consider some of the topsy-turvy things that happen in our world:

- Unborn babies are declared "non-persons" and

are denied the most basic human right: the right to life. Not surprisingly, pressure builds to use fetuses in grotesque medical experiments, and reports surface of fetal tissue being used to make, among other things, women's cosmetics (David Cannon, "Abortion or Infanticide," *Policy Review,* Spring 1985, no. 32, p. 132).

• A mildly handicapped newborn is starved to death in a hospital because its parents do not care to care for it. Medical ethicists approve the action, explaining that a newborn baby is really just a *fetus ex utero*, or "fetus outside the womb," and therefore denied the right to live.

• New York City opens a special public school for homosexual students, where they are taught and counseled how to be comfortable with their own sexuality at taxpayer expense.

• As AIDS threatens to become an epidemic, leaders shy away from denouncing sexual perversion and promiscuity, and instead try to promote "safe sex."

• As teenage suicide continues to take its tragic toll, lawyers defend the right of rock groups to "entertain" our youth with songs whose lyrics offer step-by-step instructions in how to kill yourself.

• As one commentator put it, "We live in an age where the ridicule of blacks is forbidden, where anti-Semitism is punishable by political death, but where Christian-bashing is a popular indoor sport; and films mocking Jesus Christ are considered avant-garde" Patrick Buchanan, "Commentary," *The Washington Times,* July 27, 1988).

• The same Supreme Court that forbids prayer in the public schools upholds a man's right to wear a T-shirt emblazoned with a notorious four-letter word. One commentator notes, "The Court says it's okay to use the f-word, but you can't think G-o-d" (*The Washington Times,* June 7, 1985, p. D1).

• Evidence mounts concerning the harmful effects of pornography on young people, with the parents of a twelve-year-old boy in California suing Pacific Bell for $10 million, claiming that he sodomized a four-year-old girl after hearing a "dial-a-porn" message. Yet legislators still debated whether they had the right to regulate "dial-a-porn" operations, which had made available to children disgustingly lewd messages on the family phone (*USA Today*, Hayward, California, October 15, 1987).

In recent years public awareness has been heightened regarding the need for equal treatment and opportunity for women, yet a study on pornography presented in Washington concludes that portrayals of sex "lead viewers to lose respect for women and trivialize the crime of rape." Yet a deluge of sex and "sexy" materials blankets our communications network (Deborah Wilson, "Sex Portrayal Harms View of Women, Study Says," *The Globe and Mail,* September 14, 1987, p. 1).

These are but a few examples. You can probably find several more in today's newspaper.

Nonsensical Language

On her trip through the looking glass, Alice tries

to read a poem called "Jabberwocky" written in a nonsensical language that sounds good to the ear but means nothing. We have our own form of Jabberwocky today, using nice-sounding words and phrases to describe distasteful or evil realities. We say "pro-choice" instead of killing babies. "Sexual freedom" instead of promiscuity. "Recreational drugs" instead of drug addiction. "Freedom of speech" instead of vulgarity and perversion. "Alternate lifestyles" instead of sin.

Totally confused by now? It isn't any wonder. Contradictory happenings. Irresponsible conduct. Irreverent attitudes. Illogical conclusions. Nonsensical reasoning. What is this twentieth-century land of confusion in which we live?

Pawns in a Deadly Game

Remember the chess game played in the story *Through the Looking Glass*, Alice's second trip into a strange land? Naturally the game was played in the same crazy manner in which everything else seemed to happen. But in this chess game, the pawns were alive. They were people.

Wouldn't it be terrible to be a pawn for someone else to arbitrarily move around, with no choice in the matter? Being sent here and there to serve their selfish purposes, to do their tyrannical bidding, with no concern for our welfare?

But could that very thing be happening to us? Surely we are not being used as someone else's pawns!

Or are we? Are we letting ourselves become the pawns in a deadly game with eternal consequences? Being moved around on the chess board of life not by the Red Queen but by the Prince of Darkness?

No Awakening

Our friend Alice awakened from her strange dreams. All the absurd creatures and bizarre antics were just fantasy. There was no White Rabbit, no Red Queen, no Jabberwocky, no chess game. Alice woke up to find herself safe and sound, lying on the bank of a peaceful stream.

Not so for us. We cannot just wake up as though from a bad dream. The bizarre things we have considered so briefly—and many more besides—are still happening in our world today, the world in which we must live, the world for which we each must bear a measure of accountability to the Creator.

It leads one to wonder. Why are these things happening? Where is God in all of this? What does he think about it? And what about me? Have I, like Alice, grown to accept absurdity as normal? Have I fully awakened to the dire reality of the situation? Or have I been lulled into complacency?

TWO

How Wonderful Is Our Wonderland?

There is a way which seems right to a man,
But its end is the way of death.
Even in laughter the heart may be in pain,
And the end of joy may be grief. (Prv 14:12-13)

Wonder of wonders! They had finally done it!

Barney Clark, known only to his family and friends just a short time before, was suddenly the focus of international attention. Within days his name became a household word.

Why? Because this American was the first recipient of an artificial heart. For the first time, man had built a mechanical heart and substituted it for a human heart—the most vital of the internal organs. Barney Clark lived for just a few months after his dramatic operation. But modern medicine could still credit itself with a major advance.

Hardly a week goes by anymore in which there is not some exciting new discovery or invention noted in the media. It does seem as though we live in an age of wonders.

The incredible so easily becomes credible, the unacceptable becomes accepted—not just in Alice's Wonderland, but in our own world as well. We can so easily miss the big picture of what is happening as we focus on things that press in on us personally. The old saying holds true: we miss the forest for the trees.

Our world is racing ahead at breakneck speed. But we need to ask ourselves, racing toward what? And what are the rules of this race we are in? Are there any rules? Just how wonderful *is* this modern wonderland?

Certainly there are marvelous advantages to living in this country at this point in human history: technological advances, tremendous educational opportunities, previously unimagined medical achievements, scientific knowledge—the list goes on.

But what of the inner man? What of our souls, the part of us that lives on when this brief life is ended? What of our spirits? These things are sadly neglected in the world's priorities. Yet this is precisely where the Lord would have us start: working from the inside out.

The Inner Heart

Barney Clark, and others since, have received artificial hearts. Their physical hearts have been exchanged for new ones by expert practitioners of modern medicine. But no man has ever been able to change the *inner* heart of men and women: the heart that is the seat of our being, our inner selves, our identity.

This is the heart to which the prophet Jeremiah refers when he says, "The heart is more deceitful than all else and is desperately sick; Who can understand it?" (Jer 17:9). This is the heart by which modern men and women are so greatly deceived.

And this is where the great Changer of Hearts wants to work on us. If we allow him to do his work there, it will affect everything we do and everyone we touch. The late Dr. Francis Schaeffer said it well: "The inner thought world determines outer actions."

Born to Believe

Human beings long for something to believe in, something to count on. Our Maker created us that way. God placed instincts in birds, prompting them to migrate at precise times of the year. He placed instincts in salmon, prompting them to leave the ocean waters and make their way upriver to spawn in the spring. In much the same way, he has placed within each one of us a drive to seek knowledge of himself.

Even if we do not know what causes this inner restlessness, it is there nonetheless. We feel it, like a great emptiness inside. We seek to fill it with many things: wealth, power, alcohol, drugs, sex, busyness, other people. We seek to fill it with what I call "positive pleasures," things that are not evil or harmful in themselves, but are still distractions from what is most important. Sadly, many people go through their entire lives never discovering the source of their inner hunger, and thus never able to satisfy it.

Ignoring the Instructions

Many people today are trying to correct the ills of our world. Most are probably well-intentioned. But they are attempting to repair the most complicated piece of equipment in all creation—and they have not even read the instructions!

Mankind is the handiwork of the Creator, who made us in his own image and after his likeness. Only he understands us. Only he really knows "how we work" and what to do when we "break down." His Word can give us reliable insight into our inner workings. His Spirit can do the needed repair job on the human race. Jesus, the Changer of Hearts, can succeed at solving even the most complex of our problems.

What is true on the personal, individual level is also true on the societal level. Only God knows how human society is meant to operate, and only he has the wisdom and the power to enable it to operate that way.

Our society holds a secularized worldview, fertile ground in which our enemy can plant seeds of deceit. We will examine this worldview, and the distortions it presents to us, in the pages that follow. As we do, it will become clear that this view of the world affects every facet of our lives, even as Christians. It affects the way we see ourselves as men and as women, and how we see ourselves in relationship to God and to one another.

More importantly, we will see the men, women, and children who populate our world through the eyes of our loving Father. We will look at the guidance he gives us in his love letter to all his children, the Bible.

Moral Relativism

Often the only point of agreement we can find in our modern secular society is that there *is* no moral code accepted by all. With all the intelligence we profess to have, you would think it would be easy to understand that chaos and confusion are the inevitable result of believing that truth is relative.

How did we in this country lose our moral measuring rod, anyway? Even a quick glance at the early history of the United States shows that most of the founding fathers believed in a code of moral absolutes. They established the foundations of our nation on a set of values drawn from God's Word.

While it is true that not all the founders were Christians, there *was* a Christian moral consensus in the land at that time. In fact, the opinions of those who professed to be atheists were ignored in those days, because believing that God did not exist was considered irrational! There was a firm conviction that what we believe, the value system we hold, determines how we live.

But gradually—and with ever-increasing speed in recent generations—another worldview has come to the fore. It is called secular humanism, and it takes God down from the throne and exalts man in his place.

Secular humanism is not new. As far back as the Middle Ages, and then to a much greater extent during the Renaissance and the Enlightenment man began usurping the place that rightly belongs to God. Secular humanism is a value system based upon man as the measure of all things. Autonomous. Independent. Accountable to no one for his actions.

Secular humanism is the ruling belief system of our age. While many people continue to pay lip service to Judeo-Christian values, secular humanism is clearly in the driver's seat.

"You Will Be Like God"

Satan's basic technique of temptation is the same one today that he used on Adam and Eve in the Garden. He promised, "You will be like God." Human beings are rebellious. We want to do things our way. Left to our own devices, we would very much like to "be like God," to establish our own values and determine what is right or wrong—for us. Pride, that great beguiling weakness, beckons to us all. "We'll overthrow that old, outdated, restrictive moral code," we think. "We'll set up our own. We'll be the ones in charge here."

That may sound good. But the fruit in Eden looked good, too, and it led to spiritual death. Ignoring God's laws always leads to disaster. Today we are doing things "my way" and are reaping the tragic consequences. Our social system is getting more out of kilter every day as a worldview with no room for God permeates our thinking and motivates our actions, while we fail even to recognize it for what it is. Like Alice, we too are immersed in wonderland deception.

Out of Step with Modern Times?

I experienced many pointed instances of this kind of thinking during my time of government service. Early in the Reagan administration I was a Special Assistant to the President with responsibility for liaison to women's organizations.

At that time women's issues were hot items in the media. Those in public life—and thus under media scrutiny—chose their words wisely when it came to these issues. One slip of the tongue and they could be branded bigoted, archaic, or discriminatory. Whether the accusation happened to be true or not made little difference.

Because I was known as a Christian and held views that were considered out of step with modern times, whatever I said received special attention. I was once amazed to read the reaction of some commentators when I was quoted as saying, "It is a noble thing to have the heart of a servant." I had gone on to say that women had traditionally had great servants' hearts. An innocuous statement, I thought, and certainly intended as a compliment to women.

I was astounded to see a leading business journal publish a nasty tongue-in-cheek comment about my observation, as though being a servant—giving oneself for the sake of others—was in some way demeaning, degrading, and insulting. Yet servant-hood, for both men and women, is at the heart of the gospel message. Surely we have lost our moorings if we think that behaving with humility and love for others is a thing to be avoided at all costs.

Another time a brief article about me appeared in the "People to Watch" section of the *Washingtonian* magazine. In a very cordial interview the woman reporter, knowing of my Christian faith, had asked, "Do you pray?"

"Of course," I replied.

"Do you think God hears you?" she asked.

I said, "Of course I think God hears me. If I didn't, there wouldn't be much point in praying, would there?"

When the article appeared, the headline read, "She Talks to God and Claims He Listens." How ridiculous! What interests me most is not the magazine's shallow understanding of prayer, but that they devoted a headline to the mere fact that I prayed.

We have come so far in assuming man's authority and control over life that praying to a God whom you not only believe is real but who actually listens is considered unusual enough to write about. This is in a nation where sessions of both houses of Congress, the Supreme Court, and many other official functions are regularly opened with prayer.

Religion and "Real Life"

Another clever way in which Satan has tricked us is to convince us that there must be a sharp division between the sacred and the secular, the natural and the supernatural. This belief pressures us to keep our Christianity closeted away, taken out for Sunday and funerals. Somehow, the notion that Christianity is dangerous unless limited to restricted times and doses, has become a prevailing sentiment in our society. The notion is widely accepted that religion has nothing to do with real life, anyway.

But it has *everything* to do with real life. Isn't it strange that we spend most of our time on earth concerned with things of no lasting value, things we will leave behind at death, things that "moth and rust destroy," that "thieves break in and steal" (see Mt 6:19)? Those things which possess eternal value are neglected, or at best relegated to our spare time.

But the only "things" we can take with us to heaven are other people. And the only things that will not be left behind are the treasures we have already stored up in heaven. Those treasures are stored up for us by our application of kingdom principles, by living according to God's laws in service to him on earth. The enemy would like to deny us that storehouse of heavenly treasures by convincing us that the sacred, supernatural world has nothing to do with the secular, natural world. What a tremendous lie!

A Meaningless Existence

Even with all the wonders, conveniences, and advantages of modern life, ours is still a suffering world. The age of wonders is not so wonderful after all. We have left God out of the equation of life, and the tragic results are obvious.

Without God life seems meaningless, and many choose suicide as the way out of despair. It is estimated that a million people attempt suicide each year, and about 90,000 succeed. The exact numbers are impossible to ascertain, since many such deaths are covered up or erroneously reported as accidents. Suicide is the second leading cause of death among adolescents, with more than 6,000 taking their lives yearly.

Why has human life been so devalued in our society today? Why has hopelessness crept into the thinking of so many? Because we do not acknowledge the reality of God, of a Supreme Being, in whose image we are created. When we lose this truth, we also lose the foundation for gauging the worth of human life.

As lack of respect for life grows we see more suicides, abortions, and infanticides. Now even euthanasia is coming into fashion.

The new "in" term is "quality of life." If an individual's life is determined (according to someone else's undefined standards) to lack sufficient "quality," then it is deemed expendable. Some observers warned that opening the door to abortion on demand would be but the first of many dominoes to fall. They were correct. As the old farmer said, "There's some bales of hay you just don't cut the twine on."

When we try to play God where the issue of life itself is concerned, it's like cutting the twine on a tightly packed bale. Now the hay is flying all over the place. And the mess is only going to get worse.

Why isn't our wonderland wonderful? Because "there is a way which seems right to a man, but its end is the way of death" (Prv 14:12).

Many of us, if we are honest, have also found that "even in laughter the heart may be in pain, and the end of joy may be grief." Alice woke up from her nightmare. Will we be able to shake off the shadows of the night and find a way out of our bad dreams?

THREE

The Cosmic Counterfeit

See to it that no one makes a prey of you by philosophy and empty deceit, according to human tradition, according to the elemental spirits of the universe, and not according to Christ. For in him the whole fullness of deity dwells bodily, and you have come to fullness of life in him who is the head of all rule and authority.
(Col 2:8-10, RSV)

A few years ago, millions of American television viewers watched *Cosmos*, a vivid, dramatic presentation of the mysteries of time and space. Otherworldly background music set the mood as Dr. Carl Sagan, the media's modern-day guru of scientific analysis, pronounced upon the origin and extent of space, and of life in the universe. "The cosmos," he said, "is all there is, or was, or ever will be."

Science, space exploration, and technology have brought fascinating new insights into our lives. They have engulfed our culture in a cloud of elite intellectualism. Who would presume to call into question Sagan's omission of any mention of a supreme being?

Science has become so widely equated with truth that non-experts simply are not prone to confront and challenge the flood of technical terminology and confusing data. This scientific smoke screen is one of the most effective deceits employed by the Prince of Darkness, luring us ever deeper into a contemporary distorted land of the looking glass.

The apostle Paul, in the third chapter of his second letter to Timothy, cautions us:

> But understand this, that in the last days there will come times of stress. For men will be lovers of self, lovers of money, proud, arrogant, abusive, disobedient to their parents, ungrateful, unholy, inhuman, implacable, slanderers, profligates, fierce, haters of good, treacherous, reckless, swollen with conceit, lovers of pleasure rather than lovers of God, holding the form of religion but denying the power of it. (2 Tm 3:1-5, RSV)

He urges us to "avoid such people." Why? Because "evil men and false teachers will become worse and worse, deceiving many, they themselves having been deceived by Satan" (2 Tm 3:13, LNT). Our modern scientific approach to life does not even leave room for the possibility of a Creator of the cosmos and of all who inhabit it.

Such was not always the case. Philip Yancey, in the

preface of the book *In His Image,* notes that "Up until the late eighteenth century, science was seen as a direct search for God. When Copernicus, Kepler, Galileo, and Newton made their discoveries, they believed their results taught humanity about God as well. The created world, they felt, revealed his nature" (Philip Yancey and Paul Brand, *In His Image*, [Grand Rapids: Zondervan, 1984], p. 11).

The dictionary defines "cosmos" as "the world or universe considered as an orderly system." The very orderliness of creation suggests some origin other than chance. At least that's what previous generations of scientists thought.

Sir Isaac Newton observed, "This most beautiful system of sun, planets, and comets, could only proceed from the counsel and dominion of an intelligent and powerful Being. And if the fixed stars are the centers of other like systems, these, being formed by the likewise counsel, must all be subject to the dominion of One."

A Deceptive Vision

It is ironic that many of today's scientists, so sure of themselves, have no positive, provable answers of their own about the genesis of the universe and of life itself. Although their edifice of knowledge is impressive, their theories are still just that—theories.

Modern culture, following science's lead, emphasizes those things that are provable and tangible. Seeing, after all, is believing. Yet this attitude leaves men and women totally unable to come to grips with their own frailty, old age, and inevitable death.

The essence of our being, that which lives beyond this earthly life, the ongoing part of us, is not tangible. It is spiritual, invisible to the earthly eye. A purely scientific worldview cannot deal with this crucial aspect of reality.

Indeed, such a worldview cannot possibly arrive at a purpose, a meaning, for life. What, then, accounts for the tenacity of this dead-end attitude among so many modern people? Are they simply afraid to look beyond the natural, the tangible, or are they being deceived by the Master of Deception?

The Cosmic Counterfeit

Whether we realize it or not, we are spiritual beings housed in flesh. Our yearning for spiritual things cannot be extinguished.

I am always sadly amazed when I hear about some civilized, sophisticated person who has become involved in astrology or Eastern mysticism or even Satan-worship. However, our spiritual nature yearns for spiritual truth and relationship. If we fail to enter into relationship with God through Jesus his Son, we will misdirect our spiritual quest. If we deny what's real, we end up with a counterfeit. It is precisely this spiritual vacuum, created by secular humanism, which is now ushering in the New Age movement, in which old superstitions are being given new names and dressed up for a new clientele.

I remember meeting a lovely young business-woman during a speaking tour in California. I was astounded to hear her story. In the course of her spiritual search she had gotten involved in astrology, and had become personally acquainted with many of the country's leading astrologers. She would not make a move without first consulting them.

With tears welling up in her eyes, she confessed, "Dee, I divorced my husband, whom I deeply loved, simply because an astrologer told me I should."

This beautiful, successful businesswoman had been hooked. I thank God that she later came to Christ and was set free from the control of this demonic deception. Tragically, it was too late to restore her marriage. No one had to convince her that there is real power in the spiritual realm, both on the side of good and of evil.

The Face of Evil

Several years ago I was privileged to travel to Madagascar, the large country off the southeastern coast of Africa called "The Island Continent." There I encountered a culture much different from ours. One of the long-standing cultural customs there is the worship of ancestors. This religious heritage is very much alive today, even though it is estimated that about half the inhabitants consider themselves Christians.

While in Madagascar, I was exposed to a violent reminder that the forces of darkness are indeed active today. It took place while I was in the peasant market, where many and varied items made by the local people are sold.

Madagascar is a poor country, and the poor living conditions were evident in the condition of the market. Crude wooden stalls, dirty and barely able to stay in one piece, were jammed together side by side.

As I looked at some embroidered items on one countertop, I became aware of a strange sound rising above the surrounding din.

Startled, I looked into the face of the wrinkled, dark-skinned old woman who had been trying to convince me to purchase her wares. Since she spoke only Malagasy, we communicated by facial expressions and sign language. As we exchanged glances, the expression on my face conveyed the question in my mind.

The eerie sound was growing louder now, a wild, animal-like shrieking. It was frightening, for it was clearly coming from someone totally irrational and out of control. The old woman's eyes met mine. Sensing my concern, she touched one long finger to her head, indicating that the person making the noise had a mental problem.

Or did she? Just then, running erratically down the long narrow aisle between the booths, came a young woman. There were several young children running after her, calling out in alarm. I could only assume they were members of her family. I pressed closer to the booth, trying to get as far out of the way as possible, as this tormented girl ran past. The shock of seeing the frenzied look in her eyes was surpassed only by seeing the foam coming from and covering her mouth.

I prayed for her—it was all I could do—as people scattered from her path and she ran from the market area. Was she indeed mentally ill? Or perhaps experiencing a seizure of some kind? Or was it something worse? I recalled the ancestor-worship practiced for centuries in Madagascar and the dark traditions that went with it. As the young woman's cries echoed in the distance, I experienced a deep inner awareness that demonic activity is indeed real, even in our day and age.

The Unseen World

We Christians, of course, should not be surprised that Satan is active in the world. God's Word tells us about the reality of Satan and evil spirits:

> Put on all of God's armor so that you will be able to stand safe against all strategies and tricks of Satan. For we are not fighting against people made of flesh and blood, but against persons without bodies—the evil rulers of the unseen world, those mighty satanic beings and great evil princes of darkness who rule this world; and against huge numbers of wicked spirits in the spirit world.
>
> (Eph 6:11-12, LNT)

We have come to disbelieve in the unseen spirit world around us. Even those of us who believe that the Bible is God's Word often do not want to think about the unseen world that surrounds and affects us all. Yet it is there just the same.

Dr. C. Peter Wagner, professor of church growth at Fuller Theological Seminary in Pasadena, California, has been reminding Christians of the importance of acknowledging this unseen world of good and evil forces. He calls the spiritual phenomena occurring within the Christian church today the Third Wave of the Holy Spirit. This is the name he has given to what seems to be a third major move of the Spirit in this century. The first wave was the Pentecostal movement of the early 1900s, and the second was the Charismatic Renewal movement of the 1960s and 1970s. He believes this third wave is touching many who had not been open to the Pentecostal and Charismatic movements, and to the supernatural signs and wonders accompanying them.

Signs, Wonders, and Worldviews

Dr. Wagner notes that very few of the statements of faith of American churches, denominations, and parachurch organizations mention the supernatural. One can only wonder why this is so, in light of the frequent scriptural references to these realities.

"In my opinion," he writes, "it stems mainly from our traditional Anglo-American worldview, which is materialistic and naturalistic. Secular humanism has penetrated our Christian institutions to a surprising degree.

"This is not to say that we have an atheistic

worldview," Dr. Wagner continues. "No. A large majority of Americans believe there is a God, and many know him personally through Jesus Christ. But our worldview is heavily influenced by secular science. We are taught to believe that almost everything which happens in daily life has causes and effects which are governed by scientific laws.

"God and the supernatural are much more distant to us than the average person from the Third World, for instance . . . Checking back into the New Testament, I find the worldview of the people in those days, both Jews and Greeks, was much more akin to the worldview of the Third World than to our western, secularized way of understanding reality. This is why I feel that today we need to engage in ministry like Jesus and the apostles did, expecting supernatural signs and wonders to follow" (*Christian Life*, August 1985).

When the church ignores or denies the supernatural work of the Holy Spirit, Satan is quick to come along and provide a counterfeit. Remember that man is a spiritual being who inevitably seeks out the spiritual in one form or another. This accounts for the great interest and involvement in occult practices today. They are Satan's counterfeit to prevent people from experiencing the real thing.

A Spiritual Twilight Zone

The forces of darkness are real to me and have been ever since my first exposure to the occult.

Twenty years ago I was intrigued by a friend's

experimentation with a Ouija Board. I went on to read extensively about "automatic writing" and other forms of communication with the spirit realm. At that point in my life I simply assumed that anything "spiritual" must be from God. How wrong I was! I am grateful to God for protecting me from becoming hopelessly lost in the dangerous twilight zone of occult activity.

As I discovered back then, there is a vast reservoir of material available to those interested in studying the occult. I realize now that what saved me from further involvement was the fact that the Lord knew the intent of my heart was to seek him, misguided though I was. He protected me.

Even so, in the course of my involvement I saw some strange things. Often past events were recounted with remarkable accuracy. Once a person receives accurate information about the past, he or she will assume that this same source can provide knowledge about the future. That's when they're hooked. This new source of information becomes the object of their idolatry.

God led me out of this dangerous realm and brought me to himself. If you are dabbling in the occult, even in a seemingly harmless way, you are in extremely dangerous water. Before you know it, it could be too late. Satan's goal is not to amuse you, certainly not to help you, but to destroy you.

If you doubt this, just take note of the increasing reports about satanic cults and their grisly activities. An article in *USA Today* reported that in one city animal bones and a twelve-foot cross were unearthed by sheriff's deputies tracking down reports over several months of up to 75 ritual killings of humans by a satanic cult. The dig, in an area of abandoned shacks and fields, also yielded: a headless doll wearing an armband with a satanic symbol, a knife, and hypodermic needles.

Closer to home, the popular game "Dungeons and Dragons" deals in the occult, as do a number of other popular games. Astrology is of great interest today, and books and manuals on witchcraft and Satan worship abound. Newspapers carry columns to advise you what to expect each day based on your sign of the zodiac. Some rock music encourages occult involvement and Satan worship. Parents should realize that listening to such music is anything but a harmless pastime. The consequences to their children could be life-threatening.

Twisting the Truth

One of Satan's main strategies is to persuade us, not only that God does not exist, but that he, Satan, does not exist either. Why should we be wary of someone or something we do not believe exists? Satan also offers us counterfeits of the good things our Lord has for us. Since he is not a creator, he can only distort and exploit what is already created. He takes what already exists and twists it away from its proper use.

This pattern is evident in almost every area of life, especially those realms which are mind-molders, which affect the way we view life: family, church, government, education, media, arts and entertainment, judiciary systems, medicine, business. All are subject to the enemy's assault, and all can serve as communicators of his subtle lies.

Unfortunately, the reason Satan can have such a powerful effect in so many areas is because the church, the body of believers, has not claimed these areas for the kingdom of God. Here we see the blighted fruit of divorcing the sacred from the secular, of relegating the church to one corner of society. Satan is delighted when we divide up our lives, failing to apply godly principles in every realm. In the beginning, God told Adam and Eve to exercise dominion over the earth. As his redeemed children, we likewise have a dominion mandate to apply kingdom principles and truth to the whole of human existence.

Undermining the Family

The enemy does his best to appear as an "angel of light." Some of the most dangerous of his counterfeit strategies have to do with how we raise the children God gives us.

For example, many modern people are convinced that saying no to anyone automatically shows lack of compassion. But sometimes the *most* compassionate thing we can do for someone, especially our children, is to say no to them.

Likewise, being discriminating, in the sense of being able to discern the good from the bad, is not wrong (though being prejudiced is). Standing firm in support of moral principles in the face of opposition is not being bigoted, but steadfast in character.

Dr. James Dobson, the noted child psychologist, says that it is foolish to assume that self-discipline is a product of self-indulgence. By leaving their children to flounder for moral footing, failing to provide moral guidelines and rules for proper living, many parents have abdicated their responsibilities in the name of granting "freedom" and "rights" to their offspring.

The Denial of Womanhood

The cosmic counterfeit is also strikingly evident in the area of women's issues. Certainly women have not been without grievances, having been denied many basic legal rights and economic opportunities over the years, as well as the societal recognition they deserve. However, in seeking to correct these wrongs, some women have decided they must deny their very womanhood, modeling themselves on men. Behind this approach lies the unspoken implication that men are really better than women.

Some women have felt that they have been taken advantage of as homemakers. No doubt some have. But many have mistakenly concluded that being a wife and mother is a second-class occupation. The "father of lies" (Jn 8:44) has sold us a bill of goods. What could be more important than being the mothers of humanity—the heart of the family—the ones who create the homes of the world, which are the springboards of civilization? There is no excuse, to be sure, for the lack of appreciation many women have experienced. But let's not be so foolish as to agree with those who utterly degrade the roles of wife and mother.

A distortion of truth—or even an outright lie—can take on a life of its own. Mark Twain once observed that "A lie can run halfway around the world while truth is still tying its shoes."

The new "freedom" that women are experiencing in their lives has led them into many of the same traps that men have fallen into over the years: increased alcoholism, excessive smoking (with an increasing cancer rate as a result), compulsive work habits (causing stress-related illnesses), and marriage break-ups (due to romantic involvement with others or to a self-centered quest for personal fulfillment).

Moreover, as women have sought justice and a new purpose in their lives, the role of men has also been undergoing change. While in many cases men do need to grow and change—to become more people-oriented, for example, and less goal-oriented—they should not deny their essential masculinity. The irony is that when they do, the very women who were so critical of their "macho" attitude now say these "new" men are weak, uninteresting, and wimpy.

Looking to the Source

I once heard author Josh McDowell say that we are trying to put the pieces of the puzzle of life together by looking at the picture on the wrong puzzle box.

How true! Trying to conform our lives to the world, and to the distorted image it presents of what our lives should be, can lead only to confusion and unhappiness.

In forming our view of the world, as well as in determining how we should live our lives, we must look to the only source of unchanging, eternal truth: the God who made us and to his Word.

It is clear that the Prince of Darkness has had a field day seeking to deceive us at every turn. He continues to present us with cosmic counterfeits of the truth, because he hates God and seeks to devalue, distort, and destroy those who are made in God's image—both men and women, of all ages and backgrounds.

Be of sober spirit, be on the alert. Your adversary, the devil, prowls about like a roaring lion, seeking someone to devour.

But resist him, firm in your faith, knowing that the same experiences of suffering are being accomplished by your brethren who are in the world.

And after you have suffered for a little while, the God of all grace, who called you to His eternal glory in Christ, will Himself perfect, confirm, strengthen, and establish you.

To Him be dominion forever and ever. Amen.

(1 Pt 5:8-11)

FOUR

In His Image

But we Christians have no veil over our faces; we can be mirrors that brightly reflect the glory of the Lord. And as the Spirit of the Lord works within us, we become more and more like him. (2 Cor 3:18, LNT)

What is man?

Question of questions!

This simple-sounding, yet profoundly crucial question is one that men and women have been asking since the beginning of time.

It was even asked by adventurous little Alice when everything around her—even she herself—kept changing and becoming, as she put it, "curiouser and curiouser." She asked, "Who in the world am I? Ah, that's the great puzzle!"

It is a great puzzle indeed, made more puzzling by the Master of Deceit who presents us with grossly distorted images of what we are to be like as men and women. But we must ask this all-important question. If we discover who and what *man* is, we will be better able to understand what *life* is all about and how we are to live it. We will better understand life's purpose, and *our* purpose *in* life.

Why Should Man Matter?

It is a question that the psalmist pondered long ago, as he reflected upon the majesty of God and the insignificance of man by comparison:

> I look up at your heavens, made by your fingers,
> at the moon and the stars you set in place—
> ah, what is man that you should spare a thought
> for him,
> the son of man that you should care for him?
>
> (Ps 8:3-4, Jerusalem)

It does seem strange. The God who created us and the whole universe, the God who put order in the heavens and wrote the laws of nature with such perfect rhythm and harmony, the God who sustains all things in being—*this* God is concerned about and cares for man. We stumble through life, many times ignoring God and his laws, sometimes trying to use him instead of allowing him to use us. What a strange thing indeed that God would choose to "spare a thought" for us!

Yet the reason for this divine interest in us has to do precisely with "what man is." The psalmist continues his discourse:

> Yet you have made him little less than a god,
> You have crowned him with glory and splendor,

made him lord over the work of your hands,
set all things under his feet,
sheep and oxen, all these,
yes, wild animals too,
birds in the air, fish in the sea
travelling the paths of the ocean.

(Ps 8:5-8, Jerusalem)

The reason why the God of the universe takes thought for man is because man was created in his own image. Now we can see the importance of each man and woman who has ever existed or who ever will exist. We are made in the image of the glorious God.

It seems too magnificent to imagine. Too good to be true. But true it is. And it is the key piece of information that opens the door of knowledge about what life is all about, what its purpose is—what *our* purpose is.

In the Beginning

Let's go back to the beginning. I mean the *real* beginning: the beginning of time as we know it.

It is all recorded in the book of Genesis. We are told how God created the heavens and the earth, light, water, dry land, vegetation, day and night, seasons, fish, birds, animals—he simply spoke them into being. He said, "Let there be," and there *was*. As he saw each new thing he had made, he said, "It is good."

And then . . .

> God said, "Let Us make man in Our image, according to Our likeness; and let them rule over the fish of the sea and over the birds of the sky and over the cattle and over all the earth, and over every creeping thing that creeps on the earth."
>
> (Gn 1:26)

This took place on the sixth day of creation, the final day of God's "work week." The creation of man was the capstone, the zenith of God's creation.

Take note of the pronouns used in the next verse:

> And God created man in His own image, in the image of God He created *him*; male and female He created *them*. (Gn 1:27, italics added)

Interesting! Many of us may have overlooked the implications of the wording of this account.

The story goes on to tell how God blessed them and gave them dominion over all the earth and all living things: plants, fish, birds, animals, and those things that creep on the earth. They were given dominion: told to subdue and rule over all these things of the earth.

A Suitable Partner

Let's look further. It seems that the creation of man and woman was of such importance that the story is retold, in more detail, in chapter two:

Then the LORD God formed man of dust from

the ground, and breathed into his nostrils the breath of life; and man became a living being.

(Gn 2:7)

Then something unique happens. After creating all the rest of his creation, God says, "It is good." But this time he says, "It is *not good* for man to be alone."

God determined that he would make man "a helper suitable for him." But it was obvious, as Adam surveyed and named all the living creatures that God brought before him, that none of them quite fit the bill.

So what did God do? Did he start over? Did he create Eve from scratch, from the dust of the ground? No. The Great Physician performed the first surgery!

So the LORD God caused a deep sleep to fall upon the man, and he slept; then He took one of his ribs, and closed up the flesh at that place.

And the LORD God fashioned into a woman the rib which He had taken from the man, and brought her to the man. (Gn 2:21-22)

What a beautiful gift God presented to Adam, this lovely new creature fashioned from his own rib! She was truly a part of him. And Adam knew it. Listen to what he had to say as he viewed this new, eminently suitable partner:

And the man said, "This is now bone of my bones, and flesh of my flesh; she shall be called

Woman, because she was taken out of Man."

(Gn 2:23)

Thi. then, is the starting point. If we do not understand the genesis of man and woman, then their individual worth, and their relationship to one another, can easily be misunderstood or distorted.

The story of creation gives us the answer to the psalmist's question, "What is man that you should spare a thought for him?" Man and woman are created in the image and likeness of God! They are the masterpiece of his creation. Each of us, male and female, has intrinsic worth because we are made in God's image. That is good news beyond measure!

Man and Woman

Now let us examine the creation account in order to shed some light on the conflict that has arisen about the value and significance of woman in comparison to man. Tragically, with the development of the women's movement, it is nearly impossible to address this subject objectively.

Earlier, when we looked at the pronouns used in the creation story, we saw that God created man in his image and according to his likeness; "male and female he created them." We also noted that God did not start over when he created Eve. He did not create her from the dust of the ground, but rather drew her from Adam. God took a rib from Adam and fashioned Eve from that rib. She was truly a part of him, as Adam noted when he said that she was bone of his bone and flesh of his flesh.

Note that when the Lord created Adam from the dust of the ground he breathed into his nostrils the breath of life—an action he did not repeat when Eve was brought forth. When the Holy Spirit was breathed into Adam, Eve too received the breath of life—all as part of the same action of God.

Adam and Eve, man and woman. They were one. Then they were two—and yet they were still one. We sense mystery in that, do we not?

Both Adam and Eve were created in the image and likeness of God. And it is in the fullness of what God created men and women to be individually that they will fully jointly reflect the character of their Creator. Though this is needed by men and women in marriages, certainly, this truth in no way diminishes the lives and effectiveness of singles. The need for men and women to reflect the fullness of what God created them to be is needed across the fabric of society as a whole.

We hear numerous nonsensical arguments today over whether God is male or female. It follows for some that if he has feminine characteristics, then the Bible should be rewritten with feminine pronouns used to refer to God. This seems humorous to many of us, but it is deeply tragic. For although many who speak this way are sincere and well-intentioned, it bespeaks a lack of the fear, the reverence, the holy awe, which we should have toward God, our Creator.

God is *God*. He is not a puny being, bound by

singular gender characteristics as we know them, nor by the pronouns of human language. *He is not bound.* His majesty is beyond the comprehension of these mortal minds with which we reason. We need to ask ourselves, "Do we get into these discussions because we are seeking to serve God, whom we were created to serve, or are we seeking to serve ourselves and our own point of view?"

The qualities of character attributed to God encompass the very finest characteristics made manifest in man *and* in woman. True, the pronouns used in the Bible in reference to God are masculine. Yet there are also many feminine terms used to describe him. In Deuteronomy 32 God is depicted as a mother eagle; in Isaiah 49:15 as a mother who comforts her children. Jesus likens God to a female householder seeking a lost coin (Lk 15:8-10), and even refers to himself as a mother hen (Mt 23:37). He likens the Holy Spirit to a woman giving birth (Jn 3:3-6).

Should we not ask ourselves in the first place why we seem to think that the characteristics of men are in any way of greater value than those of women? Again we see the distortion of our culture! To consider female qualities of lesser value is an error of the first order.

When we question the wisdom of God's plan for us, as we women do when we question our gender traits, our duties and privileges as mothers, the biblical blueprint for relationships in marrriage, and so on, we are really questioning the wisdom of God. That is serious business.

God has a plan, and it is a good one. It is for his glory and for our good. To follow it requires trust and faith. Not to follow it is to invite confusion and alienation.

All of us, each of us, men and women, have eternal value. We are created in the image of our Father. He decides whether to make us male or female. And he does not make mistakes!

His plan for our lives—and there is one for each one of us—requires that those traits of character which are in residence within us be brought to fullfillment. Our service to him, our service to one another, and our own fulfillment depend on it.

Sons of God?

The differences between men and women have nothing to do with our value as human beings, and certainly nothing to do with our value as sons of God. That's right, *sons* of God. Paul writes:

> For you are all sons of God through faith in Christ Jesus. For all of you who were baptized into Christ have clothed yourselves with Christ. There is neither Jew nor Greek, there is neither slave nor free man, *there is neither male nor female*; for you are all one in Christ Jesus. (Gal 3:26-28, italics added)

As Christians, we are *all* "sons" of God. We are heirs to his kingdom. That is our basic identity. Male and female denote our gender roles within that basic identity.

Before Christ, there are no differences between any of us. The ground at the foot of the cross is level. But if we, as men and as women, do not embrace our God-given gender roles and express through our lives the full character of God to the world around us, we are not going to be able to serve him fully in the calling he has given us. Moreover, we are going to deprive the world of seeing his image, reflected in the fullness of his character.

The Imperial Self

Many of us spend a tremendous amount of time and energy focusing on the negative things in our lives—or at least the things we think are negative. Most of us are blessed with such great abundance that we do not even recognize our blessings, much less show gratitude for them.

One young woman recently told me of returning to the United States after spending several months in the Middle East. "I went through culture shock when I came back," she said. "I had been living in places where just getting safely through the day was an accomplishment. Here I saw advertisements, modes of dress, and behavior that seemed utterly trivial and frivolous."

Worldly attitudes impinge upon us all. We are all touched by the secular view of life in our culture. Whether we realize it or not, we are all tainted by it in some way, to some degree.

Have you ever stopped to think how the concept

of "selflessness" has gone out of style? We are bombarded on all sides with talk of *self*-fulfillment, reaching *our own* potential, securing *our* rights. Our culture worships the imperial self.

Here again, the Master of Deception has distorted things. While these things may not be wrong in and of themselves, if they are sought and acquired at the expense of others or in disobedience to God, they are dead wrong.

How often we hear about "rights" today. Every group, it appears, is talking about its rights. Minorities, women, senior citizens, children are all clamoring for their rights. In fact, you jeopardize your own reputation for fairness if you question *any* of these demands. "Rights" is a contemporary buzzword which is perceived to equal justice. However, at times the rights of one are at the expense of another.

All of us should seek true justice. Yet the scales need to be balanced by service to others. Our Lord did not talk about pushing for our rights. He called us to serve one another. The Scriptures even urge us to *prefer* one another (see Rom 12:10).

I am reminded of a story about a church's congregational meeting. A certain parishioner repeatedly stood up and, with great emotion, spoke against almost everything. He kept charging that the church was infringing upon his rights in one way or another. His arguments were obviously unreasonable, but no one seemed to know what to do.

Finally an elderly gentlemen rose to his feet and laid the matter to rest. "My brother," he said gently,

"I would remind you that Jesus did not come to die for our rights. He came to die for our *wrongs*." That says it all.

Fixing Our Eyes on Jesus

As we have sought to bring about justice, fair treatment, and proper compensation for ourselves, we have often forgotten service and selflessness. We have placed worldly success before eternal accomplishment. We have placed products ahead of people and rights ahead of relationships.

Our situation reminds me of a "Snuffy Smith" cartoon I once saw. Snuffy is a short hillbilly character with a big nose and a floppy black hat. In this particular cartoon, Snuffy is walking along a narrow mountain trail. He has passed a sign which warns, "Watch Out for Fallin' Rocks." Snuffy is doing just that, and, with his eyes turned watchfully overhead, is about to step onto a bridge connecting one mountain ledge to another.

Unknown to Snuffy, the bridge is out. His next step is going to take him into the deep chasm between the two mountains. After noticing the first warning sign, Snuffy gave so much of his attention to watching out for "fallin' rocks" that he walked right past a second warning sign that said, "Bridge Out."

Walking through life keeping our own counsel, while trying to follow the world's signs, will lead us to the same kind of disastrous fall that Snuffy was about to take. Listening to the world, following its ever-changing cues, can distract us from listening to God. Not only that, our enemy, the Prince of Darkness, compounds the problem by distorting our vision, inviting, appealing, and cajoling us to step off the edge and plunge into the abyss.

Our only hope for making it through life on the path that leads to eternal glory is to fix our eyes on Jesus and to let his Word and Holy Spirit be our guide. If the Son of the living God, Jesus Christ, takes up residence in our hearts, we will then have that divine guide who alone can lead us safely home.

The Majestic Ones

If we could only see and appreciate our value in the eyes of the eternal God, how carefully we would walk! My heart soars when I read in the psalms the many exciting things the Lord says about his love and care for us. For example:

> As for the saints who are in the earth,
> They are the majestic ones in whom is all my delight. (Ps 16:3)

He calls us "majestic ones"! Can you imagine that God actually *delights* in us? Marvelous!

We men and women, made in the image of the God of creation, must realize that we need not— must not—be confused by the images in the looking glass that the Dark Prince holds before our eyes.

As we embrace the fullness of our God-created nature, our manhood, our womanhood, the Spirit of the Lord is free to work within us, making us more and more like God. Increasingly, we reflect the glory of the Prince of Peace—for we are his mirrors.

FIVE

In the Fullness of Time

But when the fulness of the time came, God sent forth His Son . . . (Gal 4:4)

God has a plan for all things. He has a divine timetable for the world which only he knows fully. In the book of Ecclesiastes we are told that "To every thing there is a season, and a time to every purpose under the heaven" (Eccl 3:1, KJV). The passage goes on to say that God "has made everything appropriate in its time" (Eccl 3:11).

When, in God's divine wisdom, all things were ready—"when the fullness of the time came"—he sent his son Jesus into the world. He knew when circumstances were in place for the plan of salvation, foretold in prophecy, to be fulfilled. God had this plan in mind from all eternity. And when all things were ready, God moved.

Jesus stepped from eternity into time, into the dust of this sinful world, because he loved us. No matter who we are, or where we are, or what we may have done, Jesus came because he loves *each one* of us. This is divine love, unconditional love. It is impossible for us to grasp a love so great.

It is easier for us to understand that there is an "appropriate time" for things to occur. We are accustomed to working with schedules and to laying plans—plans which require that certain circumstances be in place in order for them to work successfully.

God has a plan. He moves that plan ahead, in his great wisdom, as he discerns the time to be right.

A New Season

Very well. We might ask, then, "What about today? What time is *this* on God's timetable? Where do *we* fit into God's plan?"

Only God fully knows the answer to such questions. But I believe he gives us indications as to what his plan is, and where we fit into it, so that we will be better able to move with him in its unfolding.

I believe something is in the wind today: the wind of the Holy Spirit. That wind is blowing. The Spirit is moving.

Many people share this sense that a new season in God's plan is upon us. I hear it across the country as I speak with other Christians. I hear it in interviews in the Christian media. I read it in Christian publications.

The people who sense this move of God are Christians who seek to walk with and serve the Lord daily. Many are in the professional ministry. Some serve him in other fields of endeavor. Their vocational calls may be different, but their spiritual impressions are the same.

I sense it in my own spirit as well. God is beginning a great work in his church, in his men and his women, a work that will affect the whole world.

The Bible says, "Surely the LORD God does nothing unless He reveals His secret counsel to His servants the prophets" (Amos 3:7). God's Spirit indwells those who are spiritually born again and who walk close to him. By his Holy Spirit they are enabled to feel God's feelings and think his thoughts. They pray the prayers he puts in their hearts. They begin to discern what is on God's mind and in God's heart.

Paul reminds us, "Do you not know that you are a temple of God, and that the Spirit of God dwells in you?" (1 Cor 3:16). What a marvelous thing! What an exciting way to live! The God of the universe is in residence within our hearts.

God has positioned us, at this pivotal point in history, in a culture that is in disarray and confusion—a culture reminiscent of the land of the looking glass. He has made us his mirrors to reflect his glory to that culture. We should be both honored and humbled. But we should not be afraid.

In the World but Not of the World

The night before he died, Jesus prayed for you and for me, for all who are called by his name. He spoke to the Father about the world he was about to depart and about the followers he would leave behind.

He said to the Father, "I do not ask in behalf of these [the twelve disciples] alone, but for those also who believe in Me through their word" (Jn 17:20). Jesus was praying for all of us.

He said, "I do not ask Thee to take them out of the world, but to keep them from the evil one. They are not of the world, even as I am not of the world" (Jn 17:15-16).

Jesus prayed that we would be *in* the world but not *of* the world. How have we done? Sad to say, we have often failed. In many ways we have allowed the world to affect us, rather than affecting the world.

Called to a new Maturity

But I believe things are starting to change. Something is happening. God has started a shaking within the church, the body of Christ. He is judging the church. He is cleaning us up. He is calling us to holiness. We are being humbled. We are gaining a new awareness of the enormity of our charge, a new awareness of the need to reach out to the world around us and be salt, light, and leaven, as Jesus taught us—to influence our culture rather than be influenced by it.

God is getting serious with us. And he is calling us to get serious about him, about our faith, about our calling. He is calling us, though we remain *in* the world, not to be *of* the world. He is calling us to a new maturity, a new fruitfulness.

As a result, something is happening with God's church today. As the Spirit moves, there is a new love for one another springing up in the hearts of Christians, even though their doctrines may not completely agree.

This unity is not man-made but God-inspired. The Holy Spirit is drawing Christians together in a way that man-initiated ecumenism could never do. One minister has said that God is "throwing a great net of love over his body of believers and drawing them together." Another has said that God is "raising our tolerance level." More and more Christian leaders are coming together in the love of Jesus, to seek and to serve him *together*.

The growing unity within the body of Christ is not the only thing that is happening. There is a deepening awareness of the power of intercession, moving the heart and hands of God through prayer. All across the country the Lord is calling many to deeper prayer lives. Tremendous numbers of these prayer warriors are women.

Called to Womanhood

The Lord has called me in recent years to do a great deal of work with women, affirming them in their womanhood. I know for certain that something marvelous is happening among God's women. There is a new maturity coming. He is showing women their immense spiritual worth. He is revealing to them the enormous privilege of having been created "woman." He is calling them to a new level of intercessory prayer and power. He is revealing to them their tremendous influence in the spiritual and the natural realm.

I have been privileged to see many women whom God has used as leaders coming together in love, "preferring one another," as the Lord brings unity and healing to his body. Women are tremendous peacemakers—the "fixers" of the world.

I believe the Lord also desires to teach men how to be "men of God," and what a high call that is. As we individually, men and women, realize who we are in Christ, we will come to a greater appreciation of each other and to a greater personal fulfillment. As this happens we will become better soldiers in God's army.

Called to Boldness

Another change that is taking place is the boldness that Christians are displaying in their testimony before the world. The world has intimidated us for too long. As Peter on the day of Pentecost spoke out with a new boldness and effectiveness, we too need to proclaim Christ to a dying world, without fear or apology.

It is extremely important, however, that we not present ourselves in any way that would be a discredit to Christ. Paul offers us a caution in this regard:

Only conduct yourselves in a manner worthy of the gospel of Christ; so that whether I come and see you or remain absent, I may hear of you that you are standing firm in one spirit, with one mind striving together for the faith of the gospel; in no way alarmed by your opponents—which is a sign of destruction for them, but of salvation for you, and that too, from God. (Phil 1:27-28)

Paul says that if we *do* stand firm, without being intimidated, in a manner worthy of the gospel, in one mind and spirit, this will be a "sign of destruction" to the enemies of the gospel, and a sign of salvation to us. We need to realize that a spiritually starving world is watching us, and that what it sees has eternal consequences.

I urge you to share your faith whenever and wherever you have the opportunity. Some people say, "Oh, I could never do that. My faith is a very personal thing." Indeed our faith *is* personal. But it is not *private*. There is a big difference. The Lord tells us to go into all the world and preach the good news of the gospel.

All people, even if they will not admit it, have a need to be loved, to be important to someone. To know that there is a God who loves them unconditionally and who forgives their sins, would be the best news they could possibly receive. Do our words and actions tell them about the reality of this God we serve?

If those around us see us speaking forth our faith in love, and living it out without being intimidated, it will be a sign to them that God is real and is with us.

Unbelievers are watching us. In their hearts, they

want to believe that the story of this loving, forgiving God is true. It is up to us to make our lives into a testimony to his reality.

Marching in Step

On the trip to Madagascar that I mentioned earlier, I had another experience that stayed with me long after I left the island.

My husband and I, along with the rest of the American delegation, sat one morning in a large stadium in the national capital. The country was celebrating the 25th anniversary of its independence.

It was winter in Madagascar. Even though it never gets very cold there, the damp wind that day seemed to go right through the light raincoats we wore, chilling us to the bone.

The government was parading its military troops and equipment, with numerous delegations from around the world sitting in review. The troops marching past the reviewing stand would turn and salute their president.

Hundreds, and then thousands, of troops filled the field. It was a colorful sight, with various troops wearing the insignia of their particular unit. Each unit had a leader, someone who marched ahead and led the rest in the proper cadence. I listened as the marching bands played on for what became hours: different tunes, but always with the same insistent beat.

As I watched and listened, it struck me how just

like the world this was. The world has a drumbeat of its own. It is loud. It is pervasive. You can hear it almost everywhere you go. Sometimes you can hear little else. We become so accustomed to it that we are no longer aware of its insistent beat. Remember Alice? It all begins to seem "quite ordinary."

A Different Drummer

But surely it doesn't have to be that way, I thought, my mind rising beyond the reviewing stand where I sat huddled in my husband's raincoat. We don't *have* to march to the beat of the world's drum. We *can* march to the beat of a different drummer.

Then I realized how hard it would be for someone out on that field in front of me to march to a different beat than the one everyone else was marching in step with. It would be even more difficult if no one else but he could even hear that other drummer, or if the rest of the world refused to believe that another drummer even existed. The criticism he would receive from others, especially those closest to him, would be demoralizing.

"But," the Lord impressed on my heart, "it can be done. Think what would happen if the one marching to the beat of the different drummer marched with great confidence—if he carried himself with an air of total assurance that he was marching to the right beat."

That, I thought, was the key! What a powerful effect it would have if one person out there on that big field was marching to a different beat with utter confidence radiating in his style, his countenance, his carriage—without being intimidated by those around him.

If that were to happen, and if the Spirit of God radiated from him, before long there would be others who would start following his lead. It might only be a few at first, but one would quickly lead to another and then another and . . . before long the effect would be very noticeable.

This is precisely what we are called to do. As we move through the world around us, we are to march to the beat of a different drummer. The drummer's name is, of course, Jesus Christ.

The Dust of the World

It is extraordinarily easy to let ourselves be affected by the world around us. In my case, it wasn't until many months after I left my position at the White House and my involvement in politics that I began to realize just how much I had been affected by the world. I had certainly never denied the Lord, or lessened my commitment to him in any way. By his grace, I had been able to keep my eyes on him in the midst of some extremely difficult situations.

But something had happened to me spiritually, of which I was aware only in retrospect. Just by walking in the difficult world of politics and government day after day, the dust of the world had accumulated on my spirit. It was a fine, opaque powder, hard to discern, but it was there. I cannot really explain it, but after I left that secular life, I could tell that the dust had been there and was only later blown away by God's Spirit.

One of the reasons we can get "dusty" spiritually in the secular world is that there is generally no Christian fellowship, and no recognition given, nor reference made, to spiritual things. That is just the way it is. It is a spiritual wilderness. The effect is compounded by the demands made on our time and thoughts in the intense atmosphere common to most professions. No matter where we are called to work, it is essential that we spend time not only with the Lord and his Word, but in Christian fellowship. Fellowship is the spiritual lifeline that enables us to persevere as we march to the beat of that different drummer.

A Call From Beyond

The secular worldview is flat, without dimension, denying the spiritual life and devoid of ultimate meaning. Like Columbus sailing for the new world, we are told by those around us that we will sooner or later fall off the edge if we persist in living by our beliefs. That is certainly the perspective that the Master of Deceit would try to get us to believe. As Dr. James Dobson observes, "We are involved in nothing less than a civil war of values—a collision between two ways of seeing life" (Focus on the Family, March 1985).

A civil war of values indeed! Yet I believe good can come from it. For as the darkness gets darker, the light must get lighter. Joseph, we are told, was sold into slavery in Egypt by his jealous brothers, but ultimately was used by God to save his people. What had been intended for evil was used by God for good (see Gn 45:5-7). I believe God will do the same thing today.

A call from beyond is coming to God's church in our generation, in the fullness of his time—a call to maturity. The Master is calling us to be in the world, but not of the world. May the words of the prophet Jeremiah speak to us today:

And if you extract the precious from the worthless,
You will become My spokesman.
They for their part may turn to you,
But as for you, you must not turn to them.
                                        (Jer 15:19)

SIX

The Church Restored

But seek first His kingdom and His righteousness; and all these things shall be added to you. (Mt 6:33)

What, precisely, does it mean to "seek the kingdom of God"? How do we take dominion as God directed in Genesis? What if we find that we *have* been deceived, that the out-of-the-ordinary *has* become commonplace to us, as it was to Alice—only for us that "out-of-the-ordinary" is not just fairytale frolic but deadly reality?

I have sought for answers to these questions myself since coming to Christ, especially in the years since my husband and I came to Washington, D.C., knowing we were where the Lord wanted us, but not always sure why.

I have found, as I mentioned before, a growing awareness in the hearts of many Christian leaders that God truly is sounding a call to his people. This call is to restoration—to become a mature church, a bride without spot or wrinkle, a people that knows its position in him and in the world.

I have come to realize that it is also a call to active

duty in this world where a spiritual battle is raging. It is a battle of which many are unaware, but it is a battle nonetheless. It is about sovereignty, authority, *lordship*. It is a battle to determine who is really in charge here.

Jesus Is Lord

Talk about the lordship of Christ rolls easily off our tongues. "Jesus Christ is Lord," we say. But do we really comprehend what it means? Do we really make Jesus the Lord, the Ruler, the one in charge of every area of our lives, both as individuals and as a people? This is not to be taken lightly. Nor will it come easily. Yet it is precisely what Christ desires— what he *requires*.

Pursuing God's kingdom will lead us at times into areas that are controversial. But then our Lord was nothing if not controversial. Could we, his followers, anticipate anything else? Jesus *said* that the world would hate us. We live, as he lived, in an alien world, a world that hates truth. And he *is* truth. We are to reflect his truth, speak his truth, walk in his truth, live out his truth.

The Mind of Christ

To gain proper perspective on what is precious— what has eternal value—and on how the Lord is calling us to live, we must seek the mind of Christ. His mind is available to those who have accepted him and committed their lives to him:

> But the man who isn't a Christian can't under-
> stand and can't accept these thoughts from God,
> which the Holy Spirit teaches us. They sound
> foolish to him, because only those who have the
> Holy Spirit within them can understand what the
> Holy Spirit means. Others just can't take it in. But
> the spiritual man has insight into everything, and
> that bothers and baffles the man of the world, who
> can't understand him at all. How could he? For
> certainly he has never been one to know the Lord's
> thoughts, or to discuss them with him, or to move
> the hands of God by prayer. But strange as it
> seems, we Christians actually do have within us a
> portion of the very thoughts and mind of Christ.
> (1 Cor 2:14-16, LNT)

As we come to Christ and seek his mind, and as we
then apply kingdom principles to the whole of our
lives, we can influence history for God. We can be
part of the coming of his kingdom—his kingdom
made visible upon the earth. But to do this means
that we must submit to the lordship of Christ in
every area of **our** lives. It requires Christian maturity.

God wants his church to come of age, and is
moving by his Spirit to accomplish this in many
ways. The signs are all around, if we look—signs of
the call to maturity, to fullness, to fruitfulness. The
prophet Isaiah says, "You have seen many things, but

you do not observe them; your ears are open, but none hears" (Is 42:20). Let us beseech God to remove the scales from our eyes and the stops from our ears!

We need to listen closely for the call from beyond—his call. It is a quiet call. We get so caught up in the busyness of the world that we cannot hear it.

One morning in prayer I jotted down these thoughts I felt that the Lord had impressed on my mind: "If God is to use me as his scribe, I must come apart from the noise and clamor of the world to listen to his still, small voice of guidance. He will not turn up *his* volume to compete with the world's crashing crescendos. He is a gentle shepherd, and his sheep know his voice and listen for it. And when they hear it, they follow."

The Martyr Call

Serving the Lord, for us, is so easy compared to the price that many in other parts of the world pay for their faith. Today, in countries where there is no religious freedom, thousands suffer even to the point of death for their faith in Jesus Christ. I wonder if we in this country would stand so steadfastly in our faith if we faced such reprisals?

During our time in Madagascar Roger and I visited a church in Tananarive, the capital city. On March 28, 1848, a great act of Christian martyrdom took place there. The church is located on a high bluff, overlooking the city in the valley below. The terrain in that area of the island shifts dramatically from tabletop-flat plains to sharp outcroppings of rocky hills.

As we stood at the edge of what is called "The Hurling Cliff," gazing down to the rocks far below, the story of the courage and commitment of the early Malagasy Christians was related to us.

In an attempt to stamp out Christianity, the island's queen had ordered fourteen Christian islanders executed. They had refused to renounce their faith in Jesus Christ, even though they knew their refusal would bring certain death.

The fourteen were rolled up in woven mats and hurled over the cliff, to fall to their deaths as martyrs of the faith on the rocks hundreds of feet below.

The story is told that one of the mats became entangled in a cactus plant growing out of the side of the precipice. A soldier tried to reach down to cut it loose so the victim would continue his fatal fall. But the Christian wrapped in the mat said, "I'll do it myself." And so he did. He pulled himself loose and fell to his death—all because he was committed to Jesus Christ and would not deny his Lord.

Walking on Water

It is time for the church to follow that call from beyond and walk on to maturity, as Christ's men and women of destiny. Paul tells us that God has set apostles, prophets, evangelists, pastors, and teachers in the church in order that the body of Christ might be built up, "until we all attain to the unity of the faith, and of the knowledge of the Son of God, to a mature man, to the measure of the stature which belongs to the fulness of Christ" (Eph 4:13).

The Lord wants to use us *all* for his work. Many times he uses us to do things we never would have thought ourselves capable of doing.

I recall one such time when I was involved in a meeting where everyone else was much more professionally equipped by training and experience in ministry and Christian work than I was. Going up to my room during a program break, I lay across the bed and said, "Lord, why am I here? I'm in over my head!"

To which he responded to my heart, "Of course you are. But I want you to walk on the water. Peter was in over *his* head, too, but it was all right. He walked on the water because I said, 'Come,' and he put his trust in me. He was fine until he focused on the circumstances—on the deep water, the waves, the wind—instead of on me. If you keep your eyes on me, you can walk on the water, too."

Playing Our Part

Paul goes on, in the same passage we cited earlier, to tell us what will happen when we do come to maturity:

As a result, we are no longer to be children, tossed here and there by waves, and carried about by every wind of doctrine, by the trickery of men, by craftiness in deceitful scheming; but speaking the truth in love, we are to grow up in all aspects into Him, who is the head, even Christ, from whom the whole body, being fitted and held together by that which every joint supplies, according to the proper working of each individual part, causes the growth of the body for the building up of itself in love. (Eph 4:14-16)

How wonderful to realize that God loves us and watches over us and wants to use us! We are here not by accident, but by divine appointment. We all have a role to play in God's great drama, if only we will accept our part. This is a matter of personal decision, an act of the will. We could miss our part in this drama of eternal consequence unless we choose to accept it. If we are not to be tricked by the secular worldview and sophistication of man, nor succumb to the trickery and deceit of Satan, we simply must come to maturity and unity.

Light in the Darkness

I have begun to sense that the word "restoration" best expresses what is on the mind and heart of God in this age—restoration of his people, of his body. He wants his kingdom to become visible *through* his body, *by means of* his people. But how?

One Scripture passage that has touched me in this regard is found in the book of the prophet Isaiah:

Arise, shine; for your light has come,
    And the glory of the Lord has risen upon you.

For behold, darkness will cover the earth,
    And deep darkness the peoples;
But the Lord will rise upon you,
    And His glory will appear upon you. (Is 60:1-2)

How apt for our time! The world *is* in tremendous darkness. God is shaking the impurities out of the church. He is exposing sin. Everything that is not of the Lord is being shaken. The very foundations of societies are quaking. Everything is being called into question. Nothing is exempt. Nothing is sacrosanct.

There is thick darkness, gross darkness, over the peoples. There is confusion and distortion. The peoples of the world walk in a fantasyland, and sadly, many are willing participants in its fantasies.

But there is hope! For the Lord is coming *to* and *through* his people to fulfill his purposes. His light *will* shine upon his people, and his glory *is* going to rise upon us. He will speak to a lost world today *through us,* his body, his people.

Instruments of Healing

Not long ago I was to give one of the devotionals at the National Day of Prayer service in Washington, D.C. As I walked up to the front, my eyes fell on the Scripture verse that has become so familiar to American Christians in the last few years:

[If] My people who are called by My name humble themselves and pray, and seek My face and turn from their wicked ways, then I will hear from heaven, will forgive their sin, and will heal their land. (2 Chr 7:14)

Now, I had read that passage and meditated upon it countless times. I had seen that it is *his* people—we Christians—who must humble ourselves and pray, seeking him and turning from our wicked ways.

But on this occasion I saw something new. It struck me with full force that the healing God would send is to come *through his people.* We are to be the instruments he will use to bring healing and restoration. I shared this insight with the group assembled that day, and it has grown within me in the days that have followed.

Love Made Visible

As we noted earlier, when Jesus interceded for us with the Father on that night of his anguish, he asked that we would be one. He knew that if we were united, in a way that natural man is incapable of on his own, the world would see and take note, and would *know* that the Father had sent him. The united body of Christ would be love made visible, for Jesus *is* love.

The only way the world will ever recognize the Lord's body, and therefore know that there must be a head of that body, is if that body is united—drawn together. If there is an arm over here and a leg over there, totally ignoring (or, worse, lashing out at) one another, the body is unrecognizable. The world cannot see Jesus until the body is assembled together, united by the Spirit of love.

Two years ago the Spirit quickened me as I read the prayer of Jesus in the Garden of Gethsemane in John 17. As I reflected upon this passage, I was deeply impressed that the Father is not about to let that prayer of his Son go unanswered. Jesus would not have prayed for it if it were not possible—for with him all things are possible. It will happen. It must happen.

It is exciting to imagine how the glory of the Lord will rise upon his body—his body made visible as his glory appears upon his people! The light that will shine forth to a darkened, floundering world will draw many to itself. Healing can come to a land, a nation, a world, through the people of God.

Cleansing the Temple

If we are to be open to the work of God's Holy Spirit as he draws us to unity and brings healing to our land, we will need much personal healing and cleansing. Many areas of individual hurt and disharmony in all of us need healing, and these areas impede the Lord's work in us and through us.

Not long ago I was praying for a woman for whom I have interceded for years. She is a believer, but was not walking as close to the Lord as he would desire. I was surprised to find *anger* welling up within me. I could not understand it. I had never felt anger toward her before.

I searched the Scriptures for a passages about anger, but found nothing I did not already know: Do not let the sun go down on your anger. Be angry but sin not. And so on.

Later that afternoon the anger surged up in me again. I said, "Lord, what is this? I know you got angry, Jesus, but that was when you were cleansing the temple."

That is when it hit me.

That is precisely what he wanted to do. Cleanse the temple! *She* was the temple—his temple. "Do you not know," writes Paul, "that your body is a temple of the Holy Spirit?" (1 Cor 6:19).

The Holy Spirit was expressing through my prayer his anger at what Satan was doing to one of God's beloved. The Lord wanted to cleanse her of all those things that were displeasing to him, those things that were in the way of him using her according to the fullness of what he had planned for her.

So it is with all of us. The Lord wants to cleanse, to purge, his church. He wants to return for a church that is without spot or wrinkle. He wants to come for a mature church. One that reflects his image. One that loves one another rather than judges one another. One that has come to the fullness of manhood and of womanhood. One that is holy and seeks after righteousness. One that knows how to extract the precious from the worthless, as it unites around him, making his kingdom visible on the earth.

SEVEN

Where Sanity Begins

If you abide in My Word, then you are truly disciples of Mine; and you shall know the truth, and the truth shall make you free. (Jn 8:31-32)

How do we bring sanity back to a society that has come to accept the unacceptable, the out-of-the-ordinary, looking glass way of life?

Living in a secularized society, yet seeing life with a biblical worldview, is a whole new way of looking at things for many of us. Our minds are earthbound, and the secular humanist (man-centered) way of perceiving the world has saturated our reason and logic.

A Society Without Integrity

One evening I was at dinner with some friends—a pastor, his wife and family—who were visiting in our home during their vacation. Out of the blue the couple's eleven-year-old daughter said, "I wish my

Cabbage Patch Preemie would come alive."

The little girl's comment triggered a conversation about the popular dolls that were such a hot item in toy stores at the time. I had not heard of "preemies" before and asked her parents about them.

"I've always had reservations about the whole Cabbage Patch doll phenomenon," the father said. "The children 'adopt' these lifeless dolls—with adoption papers and everything. Now they even have them the size of premature infants, called 'preemies.' They're adopted the same way.

"It's crazy," he went on. "Children are adopting dolls on the one hand while on the other hand they watch our society killing millions of real, live human babies—the same size and supposed age as the treasured 'preemie' dolls. The irony of it! People pay a premium for these dolls and dispose of real babies. It's sick. What kind of message does that send to kids?"

He was right. It is a sick, confused message sent out to children. And I believe there is another message that resounds loud and clear, even in this one silly, distorted, situation: *Our society has lost its integrity.*

"Integrity" can be defined in a number of ways. It basically means honesty, wholeness, purity. Noah Webster's 1828 dictionary of the English language says, "Integrity comprehends the whole moral character." Integrity is *truth.*

Simply put, we have lost touch with truth—in our

personal lives and in the life of our nation. It is that simple. And what is truth? God is truth. Jesus said, "I am the way, and *the truth*, and the life; no one comes to the Father, but through Me" (Jn 14:6).

When we look honestly at our situation, and acknowledge the fantasyland condition in which contemporary society finds itself, we are required to ask, "Where does sanity begin?"

The Yardstick: God's Word

The answer must be: Sanity begins in the truth of the unchanging Word of God. His Word is the only thing that will stand firm through this life and beyond. "Heaven and earth will pass away," Jesus said, "but My words shall not pass away" (Mt 24:35). Jesus is the Word of God made flesh.

The Lord and his written Word *are* the truth. That is where we must begin. Anything less will not do. The Bible is not just an inspiring book. It is an inspired book.

In obedience to the Word of God lies the blueprint for putting our lives, our homes, our society, our nation, together with integrity. God's laws, revealed in his Word, are the yardstick against which we are to measure our lives, both individually and corporately.

God is sovereign. He is the Creator and the Sustainer of all that is. Jesus our Savior is also our Lord. His lordship requires that he reign in every area of our personal and public lives. As someone has said, "Either Jesus is Lord *of* all, or he is not Lord *at* all."

This sovereign God instituted human government in its many forms as an extension of his reign. This truth is conveyed throughout the Old Testament, as well as in the New Testament. He has instituted his delegated governmental authority in various spheres of life. It is crucial to our ability to live human life successfully that we understand and honor the government of God and pursue it with integrity.

Governing the Self

Lordship begins within each one of us, with *self-government*. If we do not have self-government, with God reigning on the throne of our personal lives as we live in obedience to his Word, we will have chaos, not only in our private lives but in our public lives as well.

Even those who do not have salvation and a personal relationship with Christ reap the benefits of a harmonious and ordered life when they apply the Judeo-Christian moral code in their lives.

One rebel can cause tyranny in a family, bring about the disintegration of a marriage, the disruption of a church, even anarchy in an entire nation. Personal freedom that is unrestricted by the protective framework of God's law will lead to anarchy. Only a people committed to self-government can make a nation based on individual liberty function with integrity.

God's Order for the Family

The government of God must also be manifested in the home.

Some women today draw back from the New Testament design for marriage relationships. Sometimes this is due simply to rebelliousness, but many times it flows from lack of understanding of God's Word and his intent. Sometimes this reluctance has developed because of abuses and errors on the part of men.

But God has established the government of the family in a wise and loving fashion. Since he is a God of order, he has established order within the family. One person is to be the head, the one who is both responsible *and accountable* for the welfare of the family.

It is the husband who is called to this role. He is to serve under, and be accountable to, Christ in this position. Chauvinism is not Christ-like. The husband is to love and care for his wife as he would for his own body—loving her even as Christ loved the church. And Christ, as we know, sacrificed his life for the church.

Willing Submission

The wife, in turn, is to *willingly* submit to her husband. She is precious—the heart of the home and of the family. The qualities that God has bestowed upon women are vital, not only to the family, but to the wider culture as well. Therefore the Lord has made protective provision for her.

There is no superiority or inferiority involved in this marriage relationship of headship and sub- mission, only mutual love and support. Both hus- band and wife are equal in worth before the Lord. Both are joint heirs with Christ of the glories of God's kingdom.

God's order for the family does not prohibit the wife from developing and using her skills and talents, so long as this does not harm the marriage relationship or cause her to neglect her respon- sibilities to her family. (The same principle, of course, applies equally to husbands and fathers.) Husbands and wives are to complete, not compete.

And, of course, Scripture tells us that children are to honor and obey their parents. They are not to "rule the roost," as so often happens in modern families. This, too, is a crucial element in God's plan for the ordering of human life.

The Church's Role

The government of God is also to be reflected in and through the church.

The church should, first of all, speak God's Word into the lives of its members, both individually and corporately, undergirding their self-government and family order.

Moreover, God's people should be the moral conscience of the nation. If the pulpits of a country are stilled, or do not uphold God's standard of moral righteousness, that nation will wander from the truth and confusion will reign.

If the church abdicates this role it forfeits its own integrity as an institution. The inevitable result is that a fantasyland mentality develops and the people become so many Alices, wandering through Wonderland, not quite sure of the proper response to the strange happenings around them.

A good case in point is the glaring moral dichotomy evident in the popularity of "preemie" dolls in the midst of an abortion epidemic. Far too many of our churches have not taken a stand against abortion. Some have actually come out in favor of legalized abortion-on-demand. They call this position "pro-choice."

I do not question the sincerity of those who support the pro-choice position. I just believe they are sincerely wrong!

How much more sane and compassionate our country would be if the church would fulfill its task of proclaiming the unchanging Word of God, the Bible, as the standard for individual and societal behavior!

The Spreading Darkness

Recently I heard Bob Mumford, an internationally recognized Bible teacher, say that darkness is coming upon the earth in an overwhelming way. He said that this darkness covers not only the religious, but also the social and the economic spheres of life.

All that is traditional in these realms is in a state of upheaval. Mumford said that people have one of three ways they can choose to turn in the midst of the kinds of changes that are taking place: to the occult, to secular humanism, or to the kingdom of God.

We can readily see how darkness has invaded so many areas of life today. Belief in the Bible as God's inspired Word has faded, and the supernatural and eternal dimensions of Christianity are often called into question.

Darwin, Marx, and Freud have affected our thinking to a striking degree. Darwin removed God from the natural world. Freud removed God from the soul. Marx removed God from government and from economics.

The Battle of Ideas

Christians, in the meantime, have had no world-view of their own, no framework of ideas and values from which to operate. We have developed splintered and fragmented ways in which we see the world. As a result, we are double-minded in many ways, unsure of what we believe or why we believe it. The world has intimidated us, and our confidence has been eroded.

We Christians have lost the battle of ideas because we have become noncombatants. We have retreated behind the walls of our church buildings. We have surrendered the realm of ideas to the so-called experts. But the "experts" are failing us. Their answers no longer hold any hope for a confused, frightened, and despairing world.

It is time for us to realize that abandoning the arena of ideas has had a profound effect upon our society; however, as it runs out of answers, the world will increasingly turn to the church looking for answers. Will the church be ready? God's Word is where we must start.

Sanity begins, righteousness begins, kingdom living begins, when we apply God's truth, acknowledge his lordship, and accept his government, in every area of our lives. Only then will we truly "abide in his Word." Only then will we genuinely "know the truth" and be set free by it.

EIGHT

A Nation Under God?

He rules by His might forever;
His eyes keep watch on the nations;
Let not the rebellious exalt themselves. (Ps 66:7)

Is America a Christian nation? Or has she become a "post-Christian" nation, as the eminent Christian philosopher, the late Dr. Francis Schaeffer, and others have contended? Was America founded on a Christian base and has she since strayed from her foundation?

America was indeed founded upon a belief in the validity of the laws of God as a moral base. There was indeed a "Christian consensus" among the architects of her government and among her citizens, even though neither group was composed exclusively of believers in Christ.

To hold to this understanding of our history is not to be a revisionist (one who rewrites history to prove a point). Rather, it is to hold to simple facts. Verna Hall and Rosalie Slater, two educators from California, have written in *The Bible and the Constitution of the United States of America*:

> In our Republic, "The church was the real morning of the state." The churches were the incarnation of Federalism for they built into the people "general intelligence, reverence for law, and faith in God." It was the pastors whose years of biblical preaching on the principles of government from God's Word lighted the way for our statesmen to clearly identify in our Constitution the precepts of the Christian idea of man and government.
>
> Charles Warren, in his *History of Harvard Law School*, writes: "It was to the clergymen that the colonists looked to guide their new governments, and in the clergymen, they believed, lay all that was necessary and proper for their lawful and righteous government. It followed, therefore, that the Word of God played a greater part in the progress and practice of the law than the words of Bracton, Littleton, or Coke."

It was customary, during the colonial period, to print and circulate the sermons of the clergy throughout the colonies and even to England. These sermons have become part of our great heritage of literature. There are still extant over a thousand of these sermons, and they represent a register of the consistency of our American Christians as they legislated, fasted, fought, and prayed their way through the American Revolution to the establishment of our Constitution (Hall and Slater, *The Bible and the Constitution of the United States of America* [San Francisco: The Foundation for American Christian Education, 1983], p. 20).

Discarding God's Law

History attests that at her founding, America had a vision. She was imperfect, and so were her founders—aren't we all?—yet America had a vision.

We have all heard the proverb, "Where there is no vision, the people perish." We may not, however, have heard the rest of the passage: "But he that keepeth the law, happy is he" (Prv 29:18, KJV). History reveals that at its founding America also upheld the standard of God's law; indeed, it was the foundation of the Constitution. John Adams said, "Our constitution was made only for a moral and religious people. It is wholly inadequate for the government of any other." (Quoted in Charles Colson's *Kingdoms in Conflict* [Grand Rapids, Mich.: William Morrow/Zondervan Publishing House, 1987], p. 47.)

Surely it is beyond dispute that America, in her brief 200-year history, has been blessed as no other nation with growth, development, advancement, and prosperity. Even with all our troubles, this remains true.

God has truly blessed our nation. Could it be because we have tried, however imperfectly, to build our system of government upon the application of his law? And could it be because of the prayers of his people that he is even now withholding his full judgment upon our nation for having discarded that law?

Merging Religion and Politics?

As more and more Christians become involved in government and the political process these days, some critics warn of grave danger in mixing God and country together.

I agree that we must exercise caution. Civil religion is never desirable. Chuck Colson, founder of Prison Fellowship, is especially sensitive to this, cautioning about the merging of religious and political views. We must never forget that the only real and lasting change takes place when hearts are changed. Jesus is the only one who can do that job. As Christians, we can be naive to the kind of manipulation that inevitably exists in the political sphere.

Colson has had firsthand experience, of course, with the failings of government. He tells of all the hard work he did when he was Special Assistant to President Nixon before the Watergate episode. Though he struggled within government to accomplish things he felt were of great value to the country, he says that things were no better—and may have been worse—when he left government service. He believes that the work the Lord has done through him since his White House years, after he gave his heart and life to Jesus Christ, has had a far greater effect on people's lives, and on the nation.

During my time in the political arena, I was saddened to see that some Christian activists seemed to be more committed to conservative politics than to Christ. Whether the allegiance is to the right or to the left, Christians simply cannot afford to lose sight of the fact that our supreme loyalty and allegiance belongs to Jesus Christ.

But while it is true that we must not make government a god, neither should we ignore it. To repeat: the basic problems of the human race lie in the hearts of men, and the solutions lie in changed hearts, not in changed policies. And yet changed hearts and the lordship of Christ within those hearts can rightly be expected to *produce* governmental involvement and change.

God instituted civil government. Godly government not only brings order, it is an instrument of blessing. But ultimately government will be godly only when godly people, committed to following God's laws, rule. Proverbs 29:2 says, "When the righteous are in authority, the people rejoice: but when the wicked beareth rule, the people mourn" [KJV].

Rights and Responsibilities of Christian Citizens

Critics of Christian involvement in the political process have received major media attention. But we must not let ourselves be confused, or intimidated into silence, by those who point to the dangers.

We need to learn, understand, and be able to explain what God's Word says about our responsibilities in the area of civil government.

The critics have said, for example, that we do not have the right to influence government with moral values. They say this would be imposing our values on others. The basic message boils down to: "It's just not fair."

Let's take a look at that statement. Common sense tells us that there is no such thing as a "value-free" piece of legislation or policy. Every piece of legislation or governmental policy is based upon *some* set of values. Why, then, should influencing government be limited to those whose values are avowedly non-Christian? That's just not fair!

Another objection is that active social and political involvement by professed Christians is not right because we live in a pluralistic society where not everyone holds the same beliefs and values. True enough.

Dr. James Hitchcock of St. Louis University reminds us that pluralistic democracy, by definition, implies conflict. Consequently it implies that political power in this nation, and hence impact on public policy, will go to the individuals who work the hardest and have the most success. Thus there is no reason for those who hold Christian values to refrain from supporting and working for things in which they believe.

Another objection to Christians applying their

values to politics and government is that doing this breeds intolerance. This view is often presented by people who are of a non-Christian faith or who have no faith at all. It is not hard to understand their concern if they do not comprehend the Christian value system. And it is not hard to see how they might be confused about Christianity, since so many times the Christian faith has been distorted, and God's Word ignored, by those who profess to be Christians. It is tragic that some great offenses against both God and man have been perpetrated in the name of Christ. Satan has been up to his tricks down through the years, and many of them have been very successful.

But the irony is that the Christian faith is the very source of tolerance. In its pure form, Christianity applied to society would bring the peace, the love, the compassion, the selflessness, the self-control, as well as the tolerance of others, that the world so desperately needs.

Great Britain's Prime Minister Margaret Thatcher at a May 21, 1988 speech, addressing the leaders of the Church of Scotland stated:

> May I also say a few words about my personal belief in the relevance of Christianity to public policy—to the things that are Caesar's? The Old Testament lays down in Exodus the Ten Commandments as given to Moses, the injunction in Leviticus to love our neighbor as ourselves, and generally the importance of observing a strict code

of law. The New Testament is a record of the Incarnation, the teachings of Christ, and the establishment of the kingdom of God. Again we have the emphasis on loving our neighbor as ourselves and to "Do-as-you-would-be-done-by."

I believe that by taking together these key elements from the Old and New Testaments, we gain a view of the universe, a proper attitude to work and principles to shape economic and social life. (*The Forerunner,* September 1988, p. 3)

One cannot have a true and honest relationship with Jesus Christ without coming to recognize the fantastic love he has for each human being, without seeing that we *all* have intrinsic value that must be acknowledged and respected. Jesus commands us to love even our enemies!

The importance of each and every person to Christ, their God-given value, and the loving nature of Jesus, are the *basis* of justice. We Christians need to be able to communicate this message.Even more important, we need to live it in our daily lives. We need to integrate our faith into every area of our lives, for Christ's sake and for the sake of a suffering world.

A Christian Nation?

Is America a Christian nation? Or at least *was* she in the past? Supreme Court Justice Brewer, who served from 1890 to 1910, wrote an opinion that established the legal logic that America is a Christian nation. He wrote:

> This republic is classified among the Christian nations of the world. It was so formally declared by the Supreme Court of the United States. In the case of *Holy Trinity Church v. United States* [143 U.S. 471] the Court, after mentioning various circumstances, added, "These and many other matters which might be noticed add a volume of unofficial declarations to the mass of organic utterances that this is a Christian nation."
>
> But in what sense can it be called a Christian nation? Not in the sense that Christianity is the established religion, or that the people are in any manner compelled to support it. On the contrary, the Constitution specifically provides that "Congress shall make no law respecting the establishment of religion, or prohibiting the free exercise thereof." Neither is it Christian in the sense that all its citizens are either in fact or name Christians . . .
>
> Nevertheless, we constantly speak of this republic as a Christian nation—in fact, as the leading Christian nation of the world. This popular use of the term certainly has significance. It is not a mere creation of the imagination. It is not a term of derision but has a substantial basis—one which justifies its use. Let us analyze a little and see what is the basis . . .

And Justice Brewer did so, making his case painstakingly and well. He concluded by saying:

> But I have said enough to show that Christianity came to this country with the first colonists, has been powerfully identified with its rapid development, colonial and national, and today exists as a mighty factor in the life of the Republic. (David J. Brewer, "America: A Christian Nation," *The Forerunner,* July 1986, pp. 12-13)

Is America a Christian nation? *Was* she in the past? Either way, the only way she will maintain her freedom and remain a land of justice and opportunity is if she is, in fact, "One Nation Under God." Helping her be such a nation is where you and I come in: by refusing to be intimidated into passivity, by standing up for what we believe in, by speaking the truth in love through the channels our political and governmental system make available to us.

Ultimately, our goal is not to turn the American and the western world back to God. It is to be faithful to Christ, to be the people of God in the midst of an unbelieving world. We are called not to success, but to faithfulness. If we are faithful, God will use us. Perhaps our country will turn back to God. Perhaps it will not. Whatever happens God will in the end prevail. We are part of his kingdom now, and we await with faith the full establishment of his kingdom which is yet to come.

NINE

Let Your Light Shine!

Again therefore Jesus spoke to them, saying, "I am the light of the world; he who follows Me shall not walk in the darkness, but shall have the light of life."

(Jn 8:12)

Great darkness has indeed overshadowed the kingdoms of this world. The land of the looking glass in which we live is shrouded in gloom. What many thought would be a land of enchantment has turned sour, and has become the land of their disenchantment.

However, there is one who brings light into the midst of it all, for he *is* light. There is one who brings sanity into the midst of insanity, for he *is* truth.

Though the darkness casts its shadow around the world, the light is growing brighter. Look again to the words of Isaiah:

Arise, shine; for your light has come, and the glory of the Lord has risen upon you.... The Lord

will rise upon you, and His glory will appear upon
you. And nations will come to your light, and
kings to the brightness of your rising. (Is 60:1-3)

Multitudes are walking in darkness in these days:
paupers and princes; the high and the mighty; the
lowly and downtrodden; men, women, and children;
old and young; black, white, yellow, and red. They
are groping along the confused, distorted passages
of today's fantasyland, looking for light to illumine
their path, to give some meaning to life; knowing not
who they are, or the great love and light there is for
them. They are unable to awaken from a dream-
turned-nightmare.

Yet all is not darkness. As God's people, we are
bearers of his light to those who walk in darkness.
We are mirrors that reflect the image of the one who
is light and truth. We are to be truly a people "called
by his name." The one who is love, who resides
within us by his Holy Spirit is the light that the
darkness cannot overcome.

Each one of us has a heavenly assignment, a divine
mission. We are to take the light of Jesus into our
homes, our towns, our businesses, our government,
and anywhere else he calls us to walk. We were
created to fulfill a purpose. Whether we serve in
full-time Christian ministry, or minister the love of
Jesus over a cup of coffee to a neighbor in the course
of our daily routine, we are here to fulfill a divine
purpose.

God's Word tells us that we are to be salt, light,

and leaven to the world. But how can we be the world's salt if we never get out of the salt shaker? How can we be the world's light if our light is kept hidden under a bushel basket? How can we be the world's leaven if we never work ourselves into the loaf? We are to touch and change our part of the world for Christ—every part of our world. Let us follow his plan for us in humble obedience.

Sheep Without Shepherds

Matthew tells us how Jesus sees those who are lost and groping in the darkness:

> And Jesus was going about all the cities and the villages, teaching in their synagogues, and proclaiming the gospel of the kingdom, and healing every kind of disease and every kind of sickness. And seeing the multitudes, He felt compassion for them, because they were distressed and downcast like sheep without a shepherd. Then He said to His disciples, "The harvest is plentiful, but the workers are few." (Mt 9:35-37)

Have you ever seen sheep running loose without a shepherd, or how sheep act when they have no boundaries of protection about them? If so, you will understand why Jesus makes this comparison between them and those human beings who flounder in confusion, wandering through life without direction and without protection.

Without a shepherd, someone to oversee them, someone committed to their welfare, sheep easily become confused. They start off one way, then stop and change direction, unsure of what to do. Several sheep may follow one of the others, whom they suppose to be the leader, only to find after a while that that sheep has turned to follow them! When trouble nears, their confusion turns to panic. They are easy prey for their enemies.

We have looked at the world around us, and have seen how many people follow these same patterns of behavior. They latch on to this or that new idea, philosophy, or psychological theory, then move on to another. Their opinions fluctuate according to the results of the latest Gallup poll. Their views on life are determined by what media report to be the sophisticated attitude of the day. The results? Despair and confusion abound. Suicide increases. Mental illness escalates.

Many today are following no shepherd. Indeed, they have no one capable of looking out for their welfare and giving them direction. They are like lost sheep, easy prey for the predator of our souls, Satan.

As we walk through life in this age, we find ourselves on treacherous ground. There are snares and pitfalls on every side. Now more then ever, we all need a shepherd to tend us. We need a shepherd to show us the way, to protect us from danger, to care for our welfare—to *love* us.

Jesus said, "I am the good shepherd." He said, "The Good Shepherd lays down His life for the sheep." He said, "I lay down My life for the sheep" (Jn 10:11, 15). And so he did. We are the sheep. That is the good news we have to share.

"The Least of These"

We have seen that God's people, if they are committed to applying his Word to the whole of their lives, can affect a nation. That is a wonderful, and much needed, truth. But we must also never forget the significance to our Lord of each individual soul, of "the least of these." We can so easily miss them. I think of one whom, sadly, I missed.

His face is etched in my memory. I saw him only once, but I shall never forget his lost and bewildered look.

My husband and I were in Paris on a Sunday morning, returning from a trip abroad. We wanted to attend church, and were given directions to a large cathedral not far from our hotel.

Entering the cathedral that morning, we were struck not only by its size and beauty, but even more so by its emptiness. There seemed to be no one there. Eventually we noticed a handful of people in a small side room. The service had started a half-hour earlier than we had been told, and was just coming to an end.

We sat quietly near the front of the cathedral. Rays of the morning sun shed a gentle light inside the quiet edifice. The tall stained-glass windows turned that light to blues, reds, greens, and golds, creating a solemn atmosphere in the sanctuary.

I prayed, contemplating the quiet beauty of the cathedral and its gloomy emptiness. Tears welled up in my eyes. To think that in a city the size of Paris this magnificent old building, erected for the worship of God, should be devoid of worshipers on a Sunday morning. I seemed to sense, in small measure, the hurt it brought to the heart of our Lord. He was there, but no one had come to be with him.

Not many had come to be with him at the cross, either, I realized. But Jesus had been there anyway— there to die for all, for those who were not present as well as for those who were. It was the same now, I thought; he was in that lonely, lovely place, even though hardly anyone else was. How faithful, how patient, he is—and how arrogant and undeserving mankind is. My heart ached for Jesus and for the suffering we still inflict upon him.

After a while we rose and made our way to the back of the church. It was then that I saw him. He was the only one left in the cavernous building. He sat as far back as he could, in the very last pew, on the inside seat next to the middle aisle. A rumpled figure in a threadbare dark suit, grimy and sidewalk-weary, he was desolate.

He sat gazing down the long aisle toward the altar, with the image of the crucified Christ hanging above it. The expression on his face was one of total helplessness. His loneliness was almost tangible. Totally oblivious to us as we filed past, his eyes were transfixed. As he stared at the figure of Christ, you could sense he was as close there in that last pew as he felt he could come. You could virtually read on his face the tortured thought: *This Jesus, this Christ, this crucified one—if he is real and if he is here, he is my last and only hope.*

I stopped and looked back at the figure huddled at the end of the pew. I wanted to say or do . . . *something.* I thought about touching his shoulder. His deepest need, of course, was for the touch of Jesus upon his heart. But maybe he also needed the caring touch of a human hand as well.

I stood there for a moment. The others were waiting, I thought. The man probably doesn't speak English, I thought. He's so filthy, I thought. I walked on, through the massive doors and out into the Paris morning.

What Is a Muddy Ruby Worth?

Later my husband said to me, "You know that man in the back of church this morning? The look on his face really got to me. I wanted to reach out and touch him. I almost did, in fact. Then I thought about what the others might think, and about how he probably wouldn't understand me, and about how terribly dirty he was. Now I could kick myself for not doing it."

I told Roger how I had had exactly the same experience, and how ashamed I was.

We blew it, plain and simple. It was obvious that the Holy Spirit had prompted us—both of us—to reach out to a brother, to a lost sheep. That ragged, lost man had little value as measured by the world's standards. But in God's economy he was of immense value. As someone once said, "What is a ruby worth? What is a muddy ruby worth?"

That man was the object of many of my prayers after that time. I pray that we never forget the lesson we learned from our encounter with him.

Reaching Out

There is such a need for all of us in the body of Christ to reach out, to allow the Lord to use us as his instruments to bring salvation, freedom, and healing to those who are in bondage.

Jesus said of the good shepherd, "He calls his own sheep by name . . . he goes before them, and the sheep follow him because they know his voice." And then he said, "I am the good shepherd; and I know My own, and My own know Me" (Jn 10:3-4, 14).

Jesus calls each of us to rely on him, to trust him, to make him an intimate part of every area of our lives. That is how the world's lost sheep will encounter their true Shepherd.

As we seek to follow after the Lord, we need to be ever mindful of the admonitions about unbelief, sin, and its consequences spelled out so vividly in Paul's letter to the Romans:

> For the wrath of God is revealed from heaven against all ungodliness and unrighteousness of men, who suppress the truth in unrighteousness.

... For even though they knew God, they did not honor Him as God, or give thanks; but they became futile in their speculations, and their foolish heart was darkened. Professing to be wise, they became fools, and exchanged the glory of the incorruptible God for an image in the form of corruptible man ... they exchanged the truth of God for a lie, and worshiped and served the creature rather than the Creator.

(Rom 1:18, 21-23, 25)

The passage goes on to say that God "gave them over in the lusts of their hearts to impurity," and recounts the depths of sin that followed. The chapter closes with these words:

Although they know the ordinance of God, that those who practice such things are worthy of death, they not only do the same, but also give hearty approval to those who practice them.

(Rom 1:32)

May God's church, God's people, those called by his very name, never be guilty of this! We need to awaken to the reality of the fantasyland of warped thinking and living around us. We need to truly humble ourselves and pray, to seek his face and turn from our wicked ways. We must bring the light of God's truth into all of life. We must not be a spectator church in a world gone mad. Repentance is needed. Intercessory prayer is vital.

"A Bunch of Amateurs and the Holy Ghost"

We *can* make a difference in our world. This fact was dramatically illustrated by a headline in the *Sunday Tribune* in Dublin, Ireland, not too long ago. It followed the defeat of a proposed law that would have allowed easy divorce in Ireland. Those believing in the moral principles of the Bible opposed and defeated the proposal against incredible odds. The media, political pundits, and legislators all thought it unbeatable.

The headline, in a liberal newspaper, was meant as an insult. But it brought great delight to the nation's believers. It attributed the defeat of the proposal to "A Bunch of Amateurs and the Holy Ghost."

That is how it all started in the upper room nearly 2,000 years ago, remember? "A bunch of amateurs and the Holy Ghost."

The Holy Spirit is moving. He is revealing Jesus to his people and to the world. As his ambassadors to our generation, we must walk in humility in an arrogant world. As Oswald Chambers cautions, "Beware of posing as a profound person; God came as a baby." This is not a time to be childish, but it is a time to remain childlike.

May the prayer of our hearts to our Good Shepherd reflect the sincere sentiments of this simple prayer, sent to me some time ago by a woman in California, whose name I do not even know:

> Lord, we are your people, the sheep of your flock. Heal the sheep who are wounded. Touch the

sheep who are in pain. Clean the sheep who are soiled. Warm the lambs who are cold.

Help us to know the Father's love through Jesus the Good Shepherd, and through the Holy Spirit. Help us to lift up that love and show it all over the land.

Help us to build love upon justice, and justice upon love. Help us to believe mightily, to hope joyfully, to love divinely. Renew us that we may help renew the face of the earth. Amen.

Impossible? For us it certainly is impossible. But absolutely nothing is impossible for God. He is the only one who can help us in the midst of this present darkness "to believe mightily, to hope joyfully, and to love divinely."